The Bonny Pirates

By VB Leghorn

Chapter 1

The clock on the wall of Ashley's English class crept along -
tick, tock, tick, tock.

Hurry up!

The **cryptic**[1] language it spoke was far too frustrating for
Ashley. How she wished she could simply **accelerate**[2] time and
make the school day be over. It was Thursday, Ashley's favorite
day of the week and she couldn't wait for the **hinderance**[3] of
having sit through one more class to be over. Her attention would
dwindle[4] by noon, **ennui**[5] would set in, and any interest in
anything but leaving school would be **discarded**[6] by the end of the
day. It wasn't that she wasn't **enthusiastic**[7] over her first year of
high school and seeing all of her friends in class (because she was).
It wasn't because she wasn't **jubilant**[8] over finding a boy that she

---

[1] cryptic (adj) having a secret or hidden meaning; (s) mysterious,
obscure; (a) clear

[2] accelerate (v) move faster; (s) speed up, expedite; (a) brake

[3] hinderance (v) any obstruction that impedes or is burdensome; (s)
barrier, deterrent; (a) help

[4] dwindle (v) become smaller or lose substance; (s) abate, decline; (a)
expand,enlarge

[5] ennui (n) the feeling of being bored by something tedious; (s) boredom,
tedium; (a) excitement, energy

[6] discarded (adj) thrown away; (s) abandoned, deserted; (a) acquired,
kept

[7] enthusiastic (adj) having or showing great excitement and interest; (s)
eager, zealous; (a) bored

[8] jubilant (adj) full of high-spirited delight; (s) joyful, elated; (a) unhappy

liked (because she was). And it wasn't because she wasn't excited to go to her job of babysitting the neighbor's **shambolic**[9] twin boys (because she didn't have to go today). It was because today was Thursday and that meant seeing her Great Aunt Tessie.

Every Thursday after school Ashley would go to see her **eclectic**[10] and **effervescent**[11] Great Aunt Tessie. Aunt Tessie lived at the other end of town and every Thursday, Ashley would visit with her and stay the night. It was something she looked forward to from the moment she left Aunt Tessie's house each Friday morning until the minute her feet were back on the front door step the following Thursday afternoon. She was so happy to stay the night with her Great Aunt because during the time with her, **feisty**[12] Aunt Tessie would expound a **narrative**[13] of fantastic tales of adventure and **sorcery**[14]. Aunt Tessie was not one to **prattle**[15] on - she recounted stories as if she had lived them - and together they would rummage through all of the hidden treasures in Aunt

[9] shambolic (adj) (British slang) disorderly or chaotic; (s) chaotic, disorderly; (a) organized
[10] eclectic (adj) selecting what seems best of various styles or ideas; (s) broad, mixed; (a) strict
[11] effervescent (adj) marked by high spirits or excitement; (s) lively, spirited; (a) dull
[12] feisty (adj) showing spirit and courage; (s) plucky, lively; (a) feeble
[13] narrative (n) an account that tells the particulars of an act or event; (s) story, tale; (a) rambling
[14] sorcery (n) the belief in magical spells that harness occult forces; (s) magic, witchcraft; (a) science
[15] prattle (v) speak about unimportant matters rapidly and incessantly; (s) chatter, babble; (a) silence

Tessie's attic. Even after all these years, they still hadn't managed to get through everything in that old attic. Aunt Tessie had spent a lifetime collecting things and things she had a plenty.

Great Aunt Tessie was a rather **sagacious**[16] woman and Ashley's favorite person in the entire world. She was a **spry**[17] one hundred and two years old, born long before cell phones or the Internet, and her **worldliness**[18] was evident. Aunt Tessie had seen so many things and been so many places. She was the most interesting person that Ashley had ever known. Aunt Tessie's husband was an **aristocrat**[19] and she was a member of an **elite**[20] group of **pedantic**[21] women with a higher education. That was almost unheard of at that time in history and these intelligent women were **peerless**[22].

She had seen **dissension**[23] between countries in a war that changed the world. She had taken part in a very important

---

[16] sagacious (adj) acutely insightful and wise; (s) wise, intelligent; (a) foolish

[17] spry (adj) moving quickly and lightly; (s) active, lively; (a) lazy

[18] worldliness (n) the quality of being intellectually sophisticated; (s) wisdom, sense; (a) naivety

[19] aristocrat (n) a member of the nobility; (s) noble, lord; (a) peasant

[20] elite (n) a member of the nobility; (s) best, top; (a) worst

[21] pedantic (adj) marked by a narrow focus on or display of learning especially its trivial aspects; (s) academic, bookish; (a) dumb

[22] peerless (adj) eminent beyond or above comparison; (s) matchless, unique; (a) mediocre

[23] dissension (n) disagreement among those expected to cooperate; (s) discord, strife; (a) peace

dispensation[24] as a donut girl in World War I. The hard-working soldiers grew tired of their usual rations of **Vienna sausage[25]**, so Tessie and a few other ladies starting making donuts from scratch and handing them out to the **ravenous[26]** soldiers. It was a unique and much appreciated task.

Aunt Tessie had unusual **acuity[27]** of being able to do anything, which made her a perfect fighter pilot in World War II where she was known to **annihilate[28]** any enemy pilots completely out of the sky. Needless to say, she was very **patriotic[29]** and a fine **ambassador[30]** for her country.

After the war, she became an archeologist who travelled the world finding mummies and treasures. Some of the stories Aunt Tessie told made Ashley believe that she may have been a secret **agent[31]** too! Her life was **serendipitous[32]**. But best of all, Aunt

---

[24] dispensation (n) the act of giving out in portions; (s) distribution, exemption; (a) denial

[25] Vienna sausage (n) short slender frankfurter usually with ends cut off; (s) hot dog, wiener; no antonym

[26] ravenous (adj) extremely hungry; (s) greedy, voracious; (a) full

[27] acuity (n) sharpness of vision; (s) acumen, keenness; (a) dulness

[28] annihilate (v) to destroy or eradicate; (s) destroy, kill; (a) save

[29] patriotic (adj) inspired by love for your country; (s) loyal, faithful; (a) disloyal

[30] ambassador (n) a diplomat of the highest rank; (s) envoy, agent; (a) yes-man

[31] agent (n) a representative who acts on behalf of other persons or organizations; (s) deputy, officer; (a) client

[32] serendipitous (adj) lucky in making unexpected and fortunate discoveries; (s) chance, lucky; (a) unlucky

Tessie was just fun to be around. She was a **spunky**[33] woman with a **tendency**[34] to look for the best in everything and always had an interesting **anecdote**[35] for any situation. Even at the age of one hundred and two, Aunt Tessie would rarely get any kind of **ailment**[36] and was still gardening, playing badminton, and writing stories.

Tick, tock, tick, tock.

The droning on of the clock was as **monotonous**[37] as the teacher's lecture.

"Miss Bonny?" The teacher was standing right next to her, her **stoic**[38] face staring down at Ashley, and she didn't even notice. Mrs. Warner was known to be completely **apathetic**[39] to distracted students. Ashley's face flushed. She had been caught being **lackadaisical**[40] when she should have been paying attention. And

---

[33] spunky (adj) showing courage; (s) bold, brave; (a) shy

[34] tendency (n) an inclination to do something; (s) bent, trend; (a) dislike

[35] anecdote (n) short account of an incident; (s) story, tale; (a) novel

[36] ailment (n) an often persistent bodily disorder or disease; (s) illness, malady; (a) health

[37] monotonous (adj) tediously repetitious or lacking in variety; (s) dull, boring; (a) exciting

[38] stoic (adj) seeming unaffected by pleasure or pain; impassive; apathetic, unemotional; (a) fervid

[39] apathetic (adj) showing little or no emotion or animation; (s) cool, indifferent; (a) curious

[40] lackadaisical (adj) idle or indolent especially in a dreamy way; (s) lazy, idle; (a) active

here she thought she was being **discreet**[41], sneaking **periodic**[42] peeks at the wall clock, but the whole room was looking at her and knew what she was doing. She looked down at her hand and realized she had drawn on it with **indelible**[43] ink the word 'bored' and quickly hid it under the desk.

"Sorry, Mrs. Warner. I was thinking." She was not trying to be **precocious**[44], she was simply being Ashley.

"Hopefully you were thinking about Shakespeare's **prose**[45]." Mrs. Warner was being **frank**[46] and her **wrath**[47] was quite evident. She had her arms crossed and she was tapping her toe.

"Yes, ma'm. It is **undeniable**[48]. I was absolutely, most definitely thinking about Shakespeare."

---

[41] discreet (adj) marked by prudence or modesty and wise self-restraint; (s) tactful, wise; (a) silly

[42] periodic (adj) happening or recurring at regular intervals; (s) regular, recurrent; (a) irregular

[43] indelible (adj) cannot be removed or erased; (s) lasting, permanent; (a) erasable

[44] precocious (adj) characterized by exceptionally early development; (a) bright, smart; (a) delayed

[45] prose (n) ordinary writing as distinguished from verse; (s) style, prosy; (a) verse

[46] frank (adj) characterized by directness in manner or speech; (s) direct, blunt; (a) evasive

[47] wrath (n) intense anger; (s) fury, rage; (a) peace

[48] undeniable (adj) not possible to contradict; (s) certain, sure; (a) moot

The classroom erupted in laughter and the boy next to her gave her a **jeer**[49]. Ashley looked around, blushing that she had blurted out something that made the entire room laugh. A crooked smile crossed her face and she laughed too. Unfortunately, Mrs. Warner wasn't laughing and Ashley could see that she was **irate**[50]. Ashley had pushed her past her patience **pique**[51].

"There has to be some **accountability**[52] here. Perhaps you can tell us the character arc for Hamlet's **monologue**[53], recite for us a **vignette**[54] or prepare a **thesis**[55] to read to the class tomorrow?"

Looking at Mrs. Warner's face, Ashley knew that nothing would **conciliate**[56] her. Normally, Ashley was an **exemplary**[57] student who could **recite**[58] many of Shakespeare's monologues

---

[49] jeer (v) laugh at with contempt and derision; (s) taunt, mock; (a) cheer

[50] irate (adj) feeling or showing extreme anger; (s) mad, furious; (a) happy

[51] pique (n) a sudden outburst of anger; (s) vex, provoke; (a) delight

[52] accountability (n) responsibility to someone or for some activity; (s) liability, blame; (a) impunity

[53] monologue (n) a dramatic composition for a single performer; (s) speech, soliloquy; (a) dialogue

[54] vignette (n) a brief literary description; (s) description, scene; no antonyms

[55] thesis (n) an essay or dissertation written upon specific or definite theme; (s) essay, paper; (a) fact

[56] conciliate (v) cause to be more favorably inclined; (s) reconcile, pacify; (a) affront

[57] exemplary (adj) worthy of imitation; (s) model, admirable; (a) bad

[58] recite (v) repeat aloud from memory; (s) repeat, tell; (a) read

verbatim[59], but this time embarrassment was **inevitable**[60]. Ashley

had not read Hamlet. She knew that Mrs. Warner was going to

reprimand[61] her in front of the whole class.

Rrrrrriiiiiinng! Saved by the bell!

"I would be **profoundly**[62] happy to...tomorrow." Ashley gave

the **obligatory**[63] smile as she gathered her books and ran from the

room, feeling lucky to **evade**[64] the **plight**[65] of answering a question

to which she didn't know the answer. Now, Ashley was not one

who was **prone**[66] to lying, but saying she would be happy to talk

about it tomorrow was a little **fib**[67]. She knew that tomorrow she

didn't have this class and by Monday, maybe the teacher would

---

[59] verbatim (adv) using exactly the same words; (s) literally, precisely; (a) inexact

[60] inevitable (adj) incapable of being avoided or prevented; sure, destined; (a) uncertain

[61] reprimand (v) an act or expression of criticism and censure; (s) lecture, scold; (a) praise

[62] profoundly (adv) to a great depth psychologically; (s) very, deeply; (a) mildly

[63] obligatory (adj) morally or legally constraining or binding; (s) mandatory, compulsory; (a) optional

[64] evade (v) avoid or try to avoid fulfilling, answering, or performing; (s) avoid, escape; (a) face

[65] plight (n) a situation from which extrication is difficult; (s) dilemma, trouble; (a) boon

[66] prone (adj) having a tendency; (s) inclined, apt; (a) defiant

[67] fib (n) a trivial lie; (s) lie, untruth; (a) truth

have forgotten to ask her again. Her **spur-of-the-moment**[68] plan

was rather **ingenious**[69].

---

[68] spur -of-the-moment (adj) occurring or done without advance
preparation or deliberation; (s) offhand, spontaneous; (a) prepared
[69] ingenious (adj) showing inventiveness and skill; (s) clever, smart; (a)
dumb

Chapter 2

Because it was Thursday, she wouldn't be meeting her brother outside for a ride home. Ben was a Freshman at Bixby College, with an **innumerable**[1] amount of friends, and he had one of the most unique cars in the world. It was an old **motley**[2], multicolored El Camino that he had fished out of a junkyard and pieced back together in a beautiful fashion while he was taking auto shop at Sunset Valley High School. Ben graduated last year and Ashley was kind of sad that they couldn't go to school together. Aside from Great Aunt Tessie, Ben was her second favorite person in the world and he was also Ashley's biggest **advocate**[3]. There was not an ounce of **spite**[4] in him. He wasn't **arrogant**[5] like many good-looking guys his age. He was smart, funny, and all the girls loved him because he was cute and nice, and wasn't at all **conceited**[6]. She was lucky to have him for a brother.

---

[1] innumerable (adj) too many to be counted; (s) countless, infinite; (a) few

[2] motley (adj) consisting of a haphazard assortment of different kinds; (s) assorted, mixed; (a) uniform

[3] advocate (n) a person who pleads for a cause or propounds an idea; (s) supporter, champion; (a) foe

[4] spite (n) meanness or nastiness; (s) malice, hatred; (a) charity

[5] arrogant (adj) having or showing feelings of unwarranted importance out of overbearing pride; (s) cocky, proud; (a) humble

[6] conceited (adj) having an exaggerated sense of self-importance; (s) vain, arrogant; (a) shy

But today was Thursday and Ashley rode her bike to school so that she could get to Aunt Tessie's **abode**[7] so much faster than walking. It wasn't far, just like everything else in the small town of Cotton Ridge, but she didn't want to waste a minute of time leaving school and getting to the house. It was the first week of school and she couldn't wait to tell Aunt Tessie all about it. She got all of the teachers she wanted - the **fastidious**[8] Miss Candy for Math, the **cantankerous**[9] Mr. Pritchard for Volleyball (her favorite **elective**[10]), and the **charismatic**[11] Mrs. Warner for Drama. All of her teachers were perfect, except for Mr. Rupert. He was **concise**[12] and **unorthodox**[13] in his teaching methods and nobody wanted Mr. Rupert as a teacher, but everyone had to have him at least once. It was an **abstruse**[14], kind of unwritten rule at the school. Mr. Rupert was an **obscure**[15] man, a **finicky**[16] science teacher who had an

[7] abode (n) any address at which you dwell more than temporarily; (s) home, dwelling; (a) public

[8] fastidious (adj) giving careful attention to detail; (s) fussy, finicky; (a) carefree

[9] cantankerous (adj) stubbornly obstructive and unwilling to cooperate; (s) crabby, cranky; (a) nice

[10] elective (n) a course that the student can select from among alternatives; (s) optional, voluntary; (a) required

[11] charismatic (adj) possessing an extraordinary ability to attract; (s) charming, alluring; (a) awful

[12] concise (adj) expressing much in few words; (s) brief, short; (a) long

[13] unorthodox (adj) breaking with convention or tradition; (s) unusual, uncommon; (a) normal

[14] abstruse (adj) difficult to penetrate; (s) obscure, puzzling; (a) clear

[15] obscure (adj) not clearly understood or expressed; (s) dim, dark; (a) clear

[16] finicky (adj) fussy, especially about details; (s) fussy, picky; (a) easy

affliction[17] when he talked - he would **slur**[18] his words as if he had a mouth full of marbles - but he was very **adept**[19] at teaching science. He had black hair, beady eyes, and brown horned-rimmed glasses that never seemed to fit quite right. His pants sat too high on his hips and his bow tie was always crooked. He was a true **erudite**[20] teacher - really smart and he thought everyone else was too. He would talk about how this **catalyst**[21] heated with that **coil**[22] would **compel**[23] that **composite**[24] to lose its **composure**[25]. It was a **comprehensive**[26] nightmare and most of the time no one could understand a word he said. He was like Einstein, only not as adorable.

---

[17] affliction (n) a cause of great suffering and distress; (s) misfortune, trouble; (a) relief

[18] slur (v) utter indistinctly; (s) blur, malign; (a) clear

[19] adept (adj) having or showing knowledge and skill and aptitude; (s) expert, skilled; (a) inept

[20] erudite (adj) having or showing profound knowledge; (s) scholarly, learned; (a) dumb

[21] catalyst (n) something that causes an important event to happen; (s) stimulus, impulse; (a) block

[22] coil (n) a structure consisting of something wound in a continuous series of loops; (s) helix; (a) untwist

[23] compel (v) necessitate or exact; (s) force, make; (a) impede

[24] composite (n) that which is made up of parts or compounded of several elements; (s) compound, blend; (a) component

[25] composure (n) a combination; a union; a bond; (s) sang-froid, imperturbability; (a) upset

[26] comprehensive (adj) having the power to comprehend or understand many things; (s) exhaustive, large; (a) parochial

The **gloss**[27] of her blue bike sparkled and she jumped on, tugged at her long, red ponytail, yanking it from where it was stuck in the Velcro **adhesive**[28] on the strap of her backpack, and headed down the **rural**[29] street. She passed the bakery on Tenth Street where the usual **entourage**[30] of cheerleaders and **rowdy**[31] football players were outside eating fresh cupcakes. They waved as she passed. She turned the corner on Pine Street and almost ran over Mrs. Jensen's **stolid**[32] cat, Whiskers, who was rolling in something in the middle of the road. Finally, she came to Maple Street where she jumped the curb at the **stodgy**[33] Mr. Hanover's driveway and raced down sidewalk to the end of the road. She tossed her bike into the grass, where the little **aerate**[34] tubes of soil and grass littered the top, and ran up the walkway that led to Aunt Tessie's door.

---

[27] gloss (adj) the property of being smooth and shiny; (s) shiny, slick; (a) dull

[28] adhesive (n) a substance that unites or bonds surfaces together; (s) sticky, gluey; (a) free

[29] rural (adj) living in or characteristic of farming or country life; (s) farm, rustic; (a) city

[30] entourage (n) the group following and attending to some important person; (s) train, suite; (a) alone

[31] rowdy (adj) disturbing the public peace; loud and rough; (s) wild, noisy; (a) calm

[32] stolid (adj) having or revealing little emotion or sensibility; (s) slow, stupid; (a) smart

[33] stodgy (adj) excessively conventional and unimaginative and hence dull; (s) dim, drab; (a) fun

[34] aerate (v) expose to fresh air; (s) ventilate, oxygenate; (a) suffocate

Great Aunt Tessie lived in a beautiful **abode**[35] in a neighborhood known for its **affluence**[36]. It was a large Victorian home, blue with white trim that had an extraordinary handmade **mosaic**[37] on the sidewalk in front of the house. It had taken Aunt Tessie many years to **amass**[38] the flowers in the large, **lush**[39] garden. It was **resplendent**[40] with many roses and other flowers, and she **maintained**[41] it with all the love of a proud mother. She had spent years on her hands and knees, **spade**[42] in hand, lovingly working each section until it was the glorious yard it is today.

The green lawn was perfectly manicured on either side of the front walkway that led to the large porch, with a standalone swing big enough for Aunt Tessie and Ashley to sit and watch the sun go down. Ashley bounded up the steps, flung open the screen door, and twisted the glass door nob. Pushing the door open, she ran inside, slamming it shut behind her.

---

[35] abode (n) any address at which you dwell more than temporarily; (s) home, house; (a) public

[36] affluence (n) abundant wealth; (s) wealth, opulence; (a) poverty

[37] mosaic (n) art consisting of a design made of small pieces of colored stone or glass; (s) tile; no antonym

[38] amass (v) collect or gather; (s) store, hoard; (a) divide

[39] lush (adj) produced or growing in extreme abundance; (s) lavish, luxuriant; (a) sparse

[40] resplendent (adj) having great beauty and splendor; (s) splendid, brilliant; (a) dull

[41] maintained (adj) kept in good condition; (s) kept, preserved (a) destroyed

[42] spade (n) a sturdy hand shovel that can be pushed into the earth with the foot; (s) scoop, shovel; no antonyms

"Auntie, I'm here!" she yelled as she flung her backpack into the corner by the old hat rack.

She was **famished**[43] and the smell of freshly baked chocolate chip cookies grew stronger as she ran into the kitchen, egging on her **youthful**[44] exuberance. There was her Great Aunt Tessie, large oven mitts covering her hands, an **anthology**[45] of recipe books from around the world lining the top of the kitchen counter, and a cookie sheet full of an **abundance**[46] of hot cookies being set atop of the stove to cool. Her hair was pulled back into a high-top ponytail with an **ornate**[47] ribbon - unusual for a woman of her age - but her white hair was still long and thick, and needed to be **tamed**[48] with a rubber band. She was usually **orthodox**[49] in the way she dressed, but always had a little something unique that would set her outfit apart from anything she had worn before. Her big blue eyes sparkled with delight as she saw Ashley enter the

---

[43] famished (adj)) extremely hungry; (s) starved, voracious; (a) full

[44] youthful (adj) suggestive of youth; vigorous and fresh; (s) young, fresh; (a) old

[45] anthology (n) a collection of selected literary passages; (s) collection, book; (a) single

[46] abundance (n) the property of a more than adequate quantity or supply; (s) lot, plenty; (a) lack

[47] ornate (adj) marked by complexity and richness of detail; (s) fancy, elaborate; (a) plain

[48] tamed (adj) brought from wildness into a domesticated state; (s) trained, subdued; (a) wild

[49] orthodox (adj) adhering to what is commonly accepted; (s) traditional, normal; (a) free spirit

kitchen. Her arms opened wide and Ashley ran into her for a big hug.

"Aunt Tessie, you made my favorites! Chocolate chip cookies!"

Aunt Tessie kissed her cheek and hugged her hard. "Of course, my dear," she said as she pulled away. Smoothing her yellow lace apron, she lifted one of the hot cookies off the tray with a metal spatula, the **brittle**[50] part around the edges sticking ever so slightly, and handed it to Ashley. "Careful now, they're hot."

Seldom[51] had Ashley been to Aunt Tessie's house and not had some kind of treat waiting for her. But Aunt Tessie was somewhat of an **anomaly**[52]. She loved to bake, but didn't particularly like sweets. She wasn't completely **abstinent**[53] when it came to sweets, but she was **abstemious**[54].

---

[50] brittle (adj) easily broken; (s) fragile, crisp; (a) strong
[51] seldom (adv) not often; (s) rarely, infrequently; (a) often
[52] anomaly (n) deviation from the normal or common order or form or rule; (s) oddity, exception; (a) usual
[53] abstinent (n) the fact or practice of restraining oneself from indulging in something; (s) celibate, frugal; (a) gluttonous
[54] abstemious (adj) sparing in consumption of especially food and drink; (s) frugal, moderate; (a) greedy

Ashley pulled apart the **unbroken**[55] cookie and watched as the gooey chocolate chips began to **ooze**[56] out of the side. Aunt Tessie went to the refrigerator, reached in and took out the milk, pouring some into a glass she had ready on the counter. She handed the glass of milk to Ashley who gulped it down greedily. Ashley wiped her mouth with her sleeve and smiled as she ate the last bite of the cookie.

"Auntie, I know what it means when you make chocolate chip cookies. It means that you have a big surprise for me."

Aunt Tessie laughed.

"You know me too well and I know you. Chocolate chip cookies **pacify**[57] even the most curious mind, but let's not speak of **trivial**[58] things. We have more important things to discuss. Tonight we open the **antediluvian**[59] treasure chest."

---

[55] unbroken (adj) marked by continuous or uninterrupted extension in space or time or sequence; (s) entire, whole; (a) broken

[56] ooze (v) pass gradually or leak or as if through small openings; (s) seep, trickle; (a) gush

[57] pacify (v) ease the anger, agitation, or strong emotion of; (s) calm, mollify; (a) excite

[58] trivial (adj) (informal) small and of little importance; (s) petty, unimportant; (a) major

[59] antediluvian (adj) so extremely old as seeming to belong to an earlier period; (s) ancient, archaic; (a) new

Ashley's mouth was **agape**[60] and she stared at Aunt Tessie's **wizened**[61] face in disbelief. This was super amazingly stupendously **colossus**[62]! Out of the extensive **aggregation**[63] of assorted items in the attic, the treasure chest was the one thing that Ashley wasn't allowed to look in and it was with unabashed **alacrity**[64] that Ashley wanted to open it. It was made of sturdy wood with metal straps that went around the top and sides. There were strange carvings in the wood, almost like the **hieroglyphics**[65] she once saw on a field trip to the museum. On the large metal latch that kept the chest secure was a pad lock the size of a grapefruit. She used to ask Aunt Tessie about the chest all the time when she was young, but the mysterious chest was off limits - to talk about and to look in. There was no **ambivalence**[66] about the fact that opening the chest was truly an **auspicious**[67] occasion.

---

[60] agape (adj) with the mouth wide open as in wonder or awe; (s) gaping, open; (a) closed

[61] wizened (adj) lean and wrinkled by shrinkage as from age or illness; (s) shriveled, wilted; (a) moist

[62] colossus (n) someone or something that is abnormally large and powerful; (s) giant, titan; (a) peewee

[63] aggregation (n) several things grouped together or considered as a whole; (s) collection, assemblage; (a) division

[64] alacrity (n) liveliness and eagerness; (s) readiness, willingness; (a) laziness

[65] hieroglyphics (n) a writing system using picture symbols; (s) character, rune; no antonyms

[66] ambivalence (n) mixed feelings or emotions; (s) doubt, uncertainty; (a) certainty

[67] auspicious (adj) indicating favorable circumstances and good luck; (s) lucky, happy; (a) ill

"Close your mouth, child. You look like a guppy," laughed Aunt Tessie and she took off her apron.

Ashley tried like crazy to **subdue**[68] her excitement, but it was impossible. She had spent years, at least a **decade**[69], in **absolute**[70] **anguish**[71] and personal **agony**[72] wanting to know what was inside of the chest, and now was the time. Why did Aunt Tessie wait so long? What were they doing in the kitchen eating cookies when they could be in the attic opening the mysterious box? She could not **ascertain**[73] what had changed to bring about the opening of the chest.

"But...but the treasure chest is off limits."

Aunt Tessie turned back to Ashely, smiled and with a great amount of **apathy**[74] said, "Not anymore. Would you like another cookie?"

---

[68] subdue (v) put down by force or intimidation; (s) suppress, crush; (a) release

[69] decade (n) a period of 10 years; (s) ten, years old; (a) year

[70] absolute (adj) perfect or complete or pure; (s) utter, total; (a) partial

[71] anguish (n) extreme distress of body or mind; (s) misery, torment; (a) joy

[72] agony (n) intense feelings of suffering; acute mental or physical pain

[73] ascertain (v) establish after a calculation, investigation, experiment, survey, or study; (s) establish, find out; (a) disregard

[74] apathy (n) an absence of emotion or enthusiasm; (s) lethargy, indifference; (a) interest

Chapter 3

"A cookie? Today is an **apex**[1] in my life and you're offering me another cookie?" Ashley was **flabbergast**[2] at the offer and that Aunt Tessie would try to **prolong**[3] the agony Ashley had endured for years waiting to open the chest. This seriously began to **agitate**[4] Ashley. Aunt Tessie could at least **acknowledge**[5] the excitement of the situation. It couldn't have been a **snub**[6], not from Aunt Tessie, but you could see the amusement on Aunt Tessie's face knowing how excited Ashley would be to open the treasure chest, and that by staying calm it was driving Ashley crazy..

"Well, you'll need your strength, dearie, for what's to come. Here, a cookie will **invigorate**[7] you." Aunt Tessie smiled.

"I couldn't eat now, even if I wanted to. I'm so excited! The **agony**[8] of waiting all these years to open the chest is finally over! I think I'm going to throw up." Ashley felt weak, nauseous and

---

[1] apex (n) the highest point (of something); (s) peak, summit; (a) bottom

[2] flabbergast (v) overcome with amazement; (s) amaze, stun; (a) comfort

[3] prolong (v) lengthen in time; cause to be or last longer; (s) extend, stretch; (a) shorten

[4] agitate (v) cause to be agitated, excited, or roused; (a) calm

[5] acknowledge (v) declare to be true or admit the existence or reality of; (s) admit, allow; (a) deny

[6] snub (v) refuse to acknowledge; (s) rebuff, ignore; (a) acknowledge

[7] invigorate (v) give life or energy to; (s) enliven, energize; (a) depress

[8] agony (n) intense feelings of suffering; acute mental or physical pain; (s) anguish, torture; (a) joy

euphoric[9] all at the same time. This whole thought of opening the chest began to **kindle**[10] her curiosity, as well as cause some **anguish**[11] about when this life-changing event was going to happen. Aunt Tessie grabbed a baggie from the counter and handed it to Ashley, trying to **abate**[12] the hyperventilation. Ashley immediately put her mouth into the opening of the bag and started breathing into it, trying to steady herself.

"You are such a **fragile**[13] girl. Just try to stay calm and don't be **foolhardy**[14]. You've waited fourteen years to open the treasure chest. You can wait another fifteen minutes." Aunt Tessie wasn't being **condescending**[15], she was simply trying to help. Aunt Tessie was always known to be rather **prudent**[16] when it came to making decisions. Not Ashley. She had been known once or twice to be **rash**[17] and make little mistakes through her **haste**[18]. This time, she

---

[9] euphoric (adj) characterized by a feeling of well-being or elation; (s) happy, elated; (a) sad

[10] kindle (v) catch fire; (s) ignite, stimulate; (a) dampen

[11] anguish (n) extreme distress of body or mind; misery, agony; (a) joy

[12] abate (v) become less in amount or intensity; (s) lessen, reduce; (a) increase

[13] fragile (adj) easily broken or damaged or destroyed; (s) delicate, frail; (a) sturdy

[14] foolhardy (adj) marked by defiant disregard for danger or consequences; (s) rash, hasty; (a) timid

[15] condescending (adj) characteristic of those who treat others with arrogance; (s) snooty, arrogant; (a) demure

[16] prudent (adj) marked by sound judgment; (s) careful, wise; (a) foolish

[17] rash (adj) imprudently incurring risk; (s) reckless, hasty; (a) smart

[18] haste (n) overly eager speed and possible carelessness; (s) rush, hurry; (a) delay

was beginning to **rue**[19] the moment Aunt Tessie told her she could open the chest.

"Nothing can be worth dying for," she said into the bag. "Breathe."

After a few moments, her breathing steadied and Ashley was starting to feel better, but she felt she was at an **impasse**[20]. The treasure chest was not a **strenuous**[21] walk upstairs and she could easily make it, even in her dizzy state, but here was Aunt Tessie forcibly keeping her here until she calmed down and ate a cookie. Ashley looked at Aunt Tessie wide-eyed over the bag, took it from her face and had a bite of the cookie Aunt Tessie was holding for her. It was still warm and gooey, and it did make her feel better.

"Can we go to the attic now?" she asked as she licked some smeared chocolate from her hand.

"Let's do. You first." It was clear that Aunt Tessie had an **agenda**[22]. Aunt Tessie had always had an **altruistic**[23] spirit when it

---

[19] rue (v) feel sorry for; be contrite about; (s) regret, lament; (a) fun
[20] impasse (n) a situation in which no progress can be made; (s) dead end, stalemate; (a) breakthrough
[21] strenuous (adj) characterized by or performed with much energy or force; (s) tough, hard; (a) easy
[22] agenda (n) a list of matters to be taken up, as at a meeting; (s) schedule, plan; (a) unplanned
[23] altruistic (adj) showing unselfish concern for the welfare of others; selfless, benevolent; (a) selfish

came to Ashley, but right now it seemed she had no intention to **cater**[24] to Ashley's needs.

Aunt Tessie let Ashley lead the way up the stairs because, although she was in good shape, her knees were a little creaky and it took her a bit to make it up the steps. Normally, Ashley was very patient with this process, but today was not a day for patience. Ashley would go a couple of steps up and bounce on her feet - heel to toe, toe to heel - waiting for Aunt Tessie to catch up. Then she would come back down the stairs and take Aunt Tessie's arm and help her up a few steps until Aunt Tessie would shoo her along again. Then she would go another two stairs and do it again. Seeing as how the attic was on the third floor, by the time they got all the way to the very top stair of the very last staircase, Ashley was about to burst with excitement.

Ashley reached out a hand to help Aunt Tessie onto the landing in front of the **quaint**[25] wooden attic door. Once her aunt was by her side, Ashley gave a hard swallow and took in a deep breath.

"Go ahead. Open the door," Tessie said in a very matter of fact tone.

Ashley opened the door and stepped into the attic, the same exact way she had done a thousand times before, except this time

---

[24] cater (v) give what is desired or needed; (s) provide, supply; (a) deprive

[25] quaint (adj) attractively old-fashioned; (s) odd, curious; (a) ordinary

instead of going to the **antiquated**[26] doll house in the corner, she headed straight for the treasure chest in the back. The **muted**[27] light coming in through the window caused a strange **aberration**[28] on the floor. The cool, musty air hit her face and the familiar smell of all the years and **myriad**[29] of oddities, many of them **obsolete**[30] memories from the past that had been packed away in the attic for decades, overwhelmed her **olfactory**[31] senses. This **convergence**[32] of sights, sounds, and smells made Ashley even more excited to see what was inside of the chest.

As she stepped over the stacks of photo albums and piles of clothes, suddenly the room changed. It became brighter. She turned in time to see Aunt Tessie, in one sweeping **motion**[33], fling open the window covering to let in the light. This was something she had never done before. The light flooded in and showed the

---

[26] antiquated (adj) so extremely old as seeming to belong to an earlier period; (s) dated, old; (a) new

[27] muted (adj) being or made softer or less loud or clear; (s) subdued, low; (a) strong

[28] aberration (n) an optical phenomenon resulting from the failure of a lens or mirror to produce a good image; (s) abnormality, anomaly; (a) norm

[29] myriad (adj) too numerous to be counted; (s) countless, numerous; (a) limited

[30] obsolete (adj) no longer in use; (s) outdated, old; (a) modern

[31] olfactory (adj) of, pertaining to or connected with, the sense of smell; (s) scent, smell; (a) odorless

[32] convergence (n) the occurrence of two or more things coming together; (s) meeting, conflux; (a) division

[33] motion (n) a natural event that involves a change in the position or location of something; (s) movement, action; (a) stillness

novelty of everything in the attic, from stuffed **mythical**[34] creatures to the wedding dress in the corner that was yellow and faded with **neglect**[35].

"You pulled back the curtains," she said turning back to Aunt Tessie. Drawing the curtains was yet another **arbitrary**[36] happening today.

"To see inside of the chest will **necessitate**[37] more light," Aunt Tessie said with a sigh. There was something different about her. She seemed older and a little tired.

It was probably just the walk up the stairs.

Ashley turned back to the attic and continued walking to the back of the room where the **anachronistic**[38] treasure chest stood waiting. She knew she was **apt**[39] to find something amazing hidden inside. Aunt Tessie followed and when she got to the chest, she reached up onto the shelf above the treasure chest, pushed

---

[34] mythical (adj) based on or told of in traditional stories; (s) legendary, imaginary; (a) real

[35] neglect (v) give little or no attention to; (s) ignore, disregard; (a) care

[36] arbitrary (adj) based on or subject to individual discretion or preference or sometimes impulse or caprice; (s) random, options; (a) deliberate

[37] necessitate (v) require as useful, just, or proper; (s) demand, need; (a) give

[38] anachronistic (adj) chronologically misplaced; (s) dated, obsolete; (a) modern

[39] apt (adj) (usually followed by `to') naturally disposed toward; (s) fitting, suitable; (a) stupid

aside a book, and **unveiled**[40] a very large, metal key attached to a rope. It, in itself, was an interesting **artifact**[41] from a time long gone. She handed the key to Ashley.

"Open it."

Ashley took the key and knelt down in front of the chest. She slipped the key into the lock and gave it a hard turn. The lock popped open and fell to the floor. Slowly, she lifted the latch and then the top.

"Wow!"

The inside of the treasure chest was a **venerable**[42] mound of **memorabilia**[43] and goods. It was filled to **capacity**[44] with a **bountiful**[45] treasure of gold, jewels, papers, and pictures. Some of the coins were very old and age had caused them to **tarnish**[46]. There was also something inside the lid. It was a large folded up piece of black cloth.

---

[40] unveiled (adj) revealed; (s) uncovered, exposed; (a) unseen

[41] artifact (n) a product of human workmanship; (s) relic, antique; (a) natural object

[42] venerable (adj) impressive by reason of age; (s) respectable, revered; (a) disgraceful

[43] memorabilia (n) a record of things worth remembering; (s) keepsakes, souvenirs; no antonyms

[44] capacity (n) the amount that can be contained; (s) size, volume; (a) emptiness

[45] bountiful (adj) producing in abundance; (s) plentiful, abundant; (a) sparse

[46] tarnish (v) make or become dirty or spotty; (s) stain, maculate; (a) clean

"Can I touch it?" Ashley said quietly.

"Of course." Aunt Tessie started to pace the floor behind Ashley. She seemed oddly nervous.

Ashley first took out a tiny chest that was on the top of the pile. She opened the little wooden top and inside were loose diamonds, rubies and other gems.

"Where did you get all of this?" she asked in **awe**[47]. Aunt Tessie smiled a **sentimental**[48] smile and turned away in deep thought, not sad or **melancholy**[49], which would have been completely unlike her, but merely thoughtful.

Ashley was **baffled**[50] by this large chest full of gold and jewels, and wondered where it came from. She turned back to the treasure chest and picked up a strand of pearls. She put them around her neck and found a matching bracelet that went onto her wrist. It was clear these were not costume jewelry, but some **opulent**[51] treasure from days gone by. All of the coins were very heavy and looked very old. The first one she picked up was dated

---

[47] awe (n) an overwhelming feeling of wonder or admiration; (s) amazement, wonder; (a) disregard

[48] sentimental (adj) marked by tender, romantic, or nostalgic emotion; (s) tender, nostalgic; (a) cold

[49] melancholy (adj) a constitutional tendency to be gloomy and depressed; (s) sad, gloomy; (s) happy

[50] baffled (adj) perplexed by many conflicting situations or statements; (s) confused, puzzled; (a) clear

[51] opulent (adj) rich and superior in quality; (s) affluent, rich; (a) poor

1701. It couldn't be that Aunt Tessie acquired all of this from just being **frugal**[52]. There had to be a story behind the treasure.

"Are these real?" she asked as she held up the coin. It glistened in the sunlight that came through the window.

"Yes, child. Very real."

Ashley reached back into the chest and pulled out another **relic**[53]. It was an old scroll, rolled to perfection with a blood red ribbon holding it in place. Her tiny hand gently pulled the ribbon from around the paper and she unrolled the scroll. Inside was a handwritten letter with a signature reading 'Love, Anne'.

"Who's Anne?" Ashley asked.

She turned around to see Aunt Tessie sitting on the cushioned chest by the window. Her face was adorned with a **serene**[54] gaze as the sun reflected off of her porcelain skin. She was staring past the trees that bobbed in front of the paned window.

"Anne Bonny. A long lost relative."

"Oh wow! She's related to us?"

"Yes."

---

[52] frugal (adj) avoiding waste; (s) thrifty, economical; (a) lavish
[53] relic (n) an antiquity that has survived from the distant past; (s) antique, souvenir; (a) new
[54] serene (adj) not agitated; (s) peaceful, calm; (a) frantic

"Did you ever meet her?" Ashley's eyes were wide with wonder. Aunt Tessie shook her head.

"No, she died long before I was born. We think it was around 1782."

Ashley reached into the chest and pulled out a picture. It was of a ship, a **gusty**[55] wind blowing at its sails. On the deck of the ship was a **gallant**[56] woman with long, dark hair that draped her shoulders. She was a **regal**[57] type of woman who could easily **elicit**[58] the respect of any man, woman or child. Her manner was not **bombastic**[59], nor was it **cavalier**[60]. It was more confident and **nonchalant**[61]. She wore a coat that looked like it was for a sailing captain and a large hat that drooped over one eye. In her hand was a sword. Ashley gave the picture a **quizzical**[62] look.

"Why does she have a sword?"

---

[55] gusty (adj) blowing in puffs or short intermittent blasts; (s) breezy, windy; (a) calm

[56] gallant (adj) having or displaying great dignity or nobility; (s) bold, brave; (a) cowardly

[57] regal (adj) belonging to or befitting a supreme ruler; (s) royal, grand; (a) average

[58] elicit (v) call forth, as an emotion, feeling, or response; (s) evoke, provoke; (a) repress

[59] bombastic (adj) ostentatiously lofty in style; (s) inflated, pompous; (a) humble

[60] cavalier (adj) given to haughty disregard of others; (s) arrogant, haughty; (a) polite

[61] nonchalant (adj) marked by casual unconcern or indifference; (s) cool, indifferent; (a) anxious

[62] quizzical (adj) perplexed; (s) questioning, odd; (a) certain

Aunt Tessie turned to Ashley and smiled a playful smile.

"Because, my dear, she was a pirate."

Chapter 4

"A pirate? We're related to pirates?" Ashley couldn't believe the **absurdity**[1] of it. Why would Aunt Tessie **fabricate**[2] such a story? Underneath that cool **facade**[3], perhaps Aunt Tessie was a bit cracked.

"We are related to a **plethora**[4] of pirates," Aunt Tessie said with a slight grin.

Ashley's thirst for more information about her family was always **insatiable**[5], but knowing that she was unique brought her to the brink of **ecstasy**[6]. Aunt Tessie grinned, showing her perfectly straight dentures and Ashley couldn't help but wonder if Aunt Tessie's mind had given way to **instability**[7]. But it had not. In fact, Aunt Tessie went on to **extol**[8] the wondrous merits of Anne Bonny.

---

[1] absurdity (n) a ludicrous folly; (s) farce, foolishness; (a) logic

[2] fabricate (v) put together out of artificial or natural components; (s) construct, invent; (a) wreck

[3] facade (n) a showy misrepresentation intended to conceal something unpleasant; (s) front, disguise; (a) interior

[4] plethora (n) extreme excess; (s) plenty; excess; (a) lack

[5] insatiable (adj) impossible to satisfy; (s) greedy, voracious; (a) satisfied

[6] ecstasy (n) a state of elated bliss; (s) happiness, joy; (a) agony

[7] Instability (n) a lack of balance or state of disequilibrium; (s) anxiety, volatility; (a) balance

[8] extol (v) praise, glorify, or honor; (s) glorify, exalt; (a) criticize

"Bonny was no ordinary pirate. She was one of the most **renown**[9] pirates ever to have sailed the high seas. Other pirates offered her **copious**[10] amounts of respect, and it was well-earned. She was quite **valiant**[11]."

"Wow! I can't wait to tell my friends. Everyone will **envy**[12] me."

"I'm afraid you can't do that. You see, I didn't show this to you until you were old enough to keep a secret and sometimes secrets can be **burdensome**[13]."

"But, I don't understand. This is the coolest thing that's ever happened to me and I can't tell anyone?"

Aunt Tessie looked out the window. Her expression was one that Ashley had never seen before. It could only be described as **torrid**[14] and Ashley was **utterly**[15] captivated by her in that

---

[9] renown (adj) the state or quality of being widely honored and acclaimed; (s) fame, celebrity; (a) infamy

[10] copious (adj) large in number or quantity; (s) abundant, ample; (a) poor

[11] valiant (adj) having or showing heroism or courage; (s) bold, brave; (a) coward

[12] envy (v) a desire to have something that is possessed by another; (s) covet, lust; (a) blessing

[13] burdensome (adj) not easily borne or endured; causing hardship; (s) hard,tough; (a) easy

[14] torrid (adj) characterized by intense emotion; (s) hot, fiery; (a) cold

[15] utterly (adj) completely and without qualification; (s) completely, entirely; (a) hardly

moment. Aunt Tessie was not one to **embellish**[16] stories and the **sincerity**[17] on her face was obvious.

"I must **confess**[18] that the general **consensus**[19] about pirates is not favorable, which is why it's always been that pirates keep their families safe by never revealing their loved ones."

"But we aren't pirates," said Ashley.

Aunt Tessie stood up and walked to Ashley. She brushed the **wispy**[20] hair back from her face and smiled at her with an **exultant**[21] look. Then she rolled up her left sleeve to reveal a tiny tattoo on the inside of her wrist, there to **commemorate**[22] her time as a pirate. It was a small skull and cross bone, and below the picture was the word 'Bonny'.

"Speak for yourself."

---

[16] embellish (v) make more attractive, as by adding ornament or color; (s) grace, adorn; (a) mar

[17] sincerity (n) the quality of being open and truthful; (s) honesty, candor; (a) hypocrisy

[18] confess (v) to acknowledge; to admit; to concede; (s) tell, reveal; (a) repudiate

[19] consensus (n) agreement in the judgment or opinion reached by a group as a whole; (s) consent, unity; (a) argument

[20] wispy (adj) thin and weak; (s) frail, slender; (a) strong

[21] exultant (adj) joyful and proud especially because of triumph or success; (s) happy, joyful; (a) sad

[22] commemorate (v) call to remembrance; (s) celebrate, mark; (a) neglect

Ashley let out an **audible**[23] gasp as Aunt Tessie began to roll back down her sleeve. She couldn't believe that in all of these years Aunt Tessie didn't **confide**[24] in her before. In fact, in that moment Ashley realized she had never seen Aunt Tessie in a short-sleeved shirt. All of this was coming together - the treasure, the secrets, Aunt Tessie. This wonderful, **vibrant**[25] woman that Ashley had known her whole life - loved and respected - was a pirate!

"You were a pirate?" Ashley's mouth was wide open and her eyes were as big as saucers.

"I am a pirate. Let me **reiterate**[26]. Once a pirate, always a pirate." Aunt Tessie stood up and paced the room. "Now remember, you must be **discreet**[27] about this. Our very existence depends on it."

"Why did you do it?"

Aunt Tessie laughed. "Well, **despite**[28] what you may have read, pirates aren't all bad. It wasn't **aggrandizement**[29]. It was family

---

[23] audible (adj) heard or perceptible by the ear; (s) clear, audio; (a) silent
[24] confide (v) reveal in private; (s) entrust, tell; (a) conceal
[25] vibrant (adj) vigorous and animated; (s) lively, active; (a) dull
[26] reiterate (v) say, state, or perform again; (s) repeat, echo; (a) conceal
[27] discreet (adj) marked by prudence or modesty and wise self-restraint; (s) wary, cautious; (a) foolish
[28] despite (prep) In spite of; against or in defiance of; notwithstanding; (s) even though, in spite of; (a) exalt
[29] aggrandizement (n) perks, growth; (a) floccinaucinihilipilification

pride, an **allegiance**[30] to who we are. I wanted to carry on the tradition."

Ashley wasn't sure whether to be excited or **appalled**[31].

"Did you pillage and **plunder**[32]? Did you ever **abduct**[33] someone? Did the police ever **apprehend**[34] you?"

"Don't be **cliche**[35]. I would never have been one of those **vile**[36] pirates that would lower themselves to hurting someone. A good pirate doesn't **condone**[37] those actions, but being a pirate is **conducive**[38] to certain things. Let's just say that I did what pirates do best and I was very good at it."

"What kind of a pirate were you?"

---

[30] allegiance (n) the act of binding yourself to a course of action; (s) loyalty, fidelity; (a) treason

[31] appalled (adj) struck with fear, dread, or consternation; (s) aghast, shocked; (a) brave

[32] plunder (v) steal goods; take as spoils; (s) loot, pillage; (a) give

[33] abduct (v) take away to an undisclosed location against their will; (s) kidnap, seize; (a) release

[34] apprehend (v) take into custody; (s) catch, arrest; (a) lose

[35] cliche (n) a trite or obvious remark; (s) banality, platitude; (a) neologism

[36] vile (adj) morally reprehensible; (s) foul, nasty; (a) lovely

[37] condone (adj) excuse, overlook, or make allowances for; (s) allow, pardon; (a) forbid

[38] conducive (adj) tending to bring about; being partly responsible for; (s) helpful, beneficial; (a) muddle

Aunt Tessie thought for only a **slight**[39] moment. "I was not **brash**[40], but I was very **astute**[41]. I was not **atrocious**[42], but perhaps a bit **zany**[43]. I was **ominous**[44] when need be, seldom **timid**[45] and never **somber**[46]. I was usually **congenial**[47], a lot **controversial**[48], but always polite. I guess you could say I was a **wholesome**[49] pirate."

Ashley looked down at the treasure chest. She could not **avert**[50] her eyes from the beauty of the treasure. Inside, she saw a small book with a red leather cover. She reached in and lifted it out. She opened the tiny book and there inside, on the first page, was a picture of another lady pirate. She was majestic and proud, standing on the bow of a ship with her hand on the hilt of a sword

---

[39] slight (adj) small in quantity or degree; (s) small, little; (a) big

[40] brash (adj) offensively bold; (s) cheeky, brazen; (a) shy

[41] astute (adj) marked by practical hardheaded intelligence; (s) clever, sharp; (a) stupid

[42] atrocious (adj) shockingly brutal or cruel; (s) awful, terrible; (a) kind

[43] zany (adj) ludicrous or foolish; (s) goofy, crazy; (a) sensible

[44] ominous (adj) threatening or foreshadowing evil or tragic developments; (s) scary, grim; (a) bright

[45] timid (adj) showing fear and lack of courage; (s) shy,bashful; (a) brave

[46] somber (adj) grave or even gloomy in character; (s) dreary, dismal; (a) cheerful

[47] congenial (adj) suitable to your needs; (s) pleasant, friendly; (a) harsh

[48] controversial (adj) marked by or capable of arousing disagreement; (s) moot, contentious; (a) peaceful

[49] wholesome (adj) conducive to or characteristic of physical or moral well-being; (s) good, clean; (a) bad

[50] avert (v) turn away or aside; (s) avoid, divert; (a) take a look

that was fastened in a sheath that hung on a belt around her waist. In her hat was a large red **plume**[51]. Ashley knew the face at once.

"This is you," Ashley whispered in a softened voice.

She turned to the next page and read the bold words that were on the page.

"A Pirate's Tale. By Tess Bonny. That's you!" exclaimed Ashley. Aunt Tessie nodded.

Now, at this point Ashley wasn't sure what to say. It was completely **implausible**[52] that Ashley was related to pirates and she was trying to **grapple**[53] with this reality. This had to be some crazy **hyperbole**[54] devised by Aunt Tessie to test her. She had a hundred questions running through her head and needed answers to every, single one. But what came next was only going to bring up more questions.

---

[51] plume (n) the feather of a bird; (s) quill, fleece; (a) deprecate

[52] implausible (adj) highly imaginative but unlikely; (s) incredible, improbable; (a) likely

[53] grapple (v) work hard to come to terms with or deal with something; (s) grasp, grip; (a) release

[54] hyperbole (n) extravagant exaggeration; (s) puffery, metaphor; (a) litotes

"I'm getting old, downright **archaic**[55]," said Aunt Tessie. "And it's time for me to **abdicate**[56] my position as the lead pirate in the family, for me to **appoint**[57] another leader, and for our legacy to continue with someone else. As a pirate, I can only live **vicariously**[58] now through another. I have made a **chronicle**[59] of my adventures, one that will **illuminate**[60] everything about the **hereditary**[61] pirate lifestyle. It is tradition to pass along the Bonny treasure to each next generation of **authentic**[62] Bonny pirates. I am the **benefactor**[63] and it's now your turn to receive the treasure."

---

[55] archaic (adj) so extremely old as seeming to belong to an earlier period; (s) old, obsolete; (a) new

[56] abdicate (v) give up, such as power, as of monarchs and emperors; (s) quit, resign; (a) claim

[57] appoint (v) assign a duty, responsibility or obligation to; (s) name, designate; (a) dismiss

[58] vicariously (adv) indirectly, as, by, or through a substitute; (s) indirectly, proxy; no antonyms

[59] chronicle (n) a record or narrative description of past events; (s) story, diary; (a) secret

[60] illuminate (v) make lighter or brighter; (s) enlighten, clarify; (a) confuse

[61] hereditary (adj) occurring among people descended from a common ancestor; (s) native, innate; (a) new

[62] authentic (adj) not counterfeit or copied; (s) true, real; (a) fake

[63] benefactor (n) one who confers a benefit or benefits; (s) guardian, champion; (a) foe

Chapter 5

Ashley made a face. "My turn? But I'm not a pirate."

"You are by blood and that's what counts. But the treasure isn't simply handed to you. You must **prove**[1] yourself and earn it."

"I'm not athletic at all. You know that."

"You're not **infirm**[2] either. You know that."

Aunt Tessie took the red book from Ashley and opened it to the last page where there was an **epilogue**[3] and a paper stuck to the back cover.

"I have hidden a treasure for you to find. This map, along with other things, will lead you there. Just like the Bonny Pirate before me and the Bonny Pirate before her, once you find the treasure, you will become the next Bonny Pirate."

Ashley was thoroughly **bemused**[4]. "You want me to be your **apprentice**[5]? But I'm only fourteen and I can't sail."

---

[1] prove (v) establish the validity of something; (demonstrate, show; (a) confute

[2] infirm (adj) lacking bodily or muscular strength or vitality; (s) invalid, disabled; (a) strong

[3] epilogue (n) a short passage added at the end of a literary work; (s) conclusion, finale; (a) preface

[4] bemused (adj) perplexed by many conflicting situations or statements; (s) baffled, lost; (a) alert

[5] apprentice (n) someone who works for an expert to learn a trade; (s) student, learner; (a) master

Aunt Tessie was **brimming**[6] with laughter. "You don't have to sail a pirate ship or wear an eye patch. You simply have to carry on the dream. You have the **authority**[7]. You can do that."

Ashley was **conscientious**[8], but never an overly confident girl. She knew she was capable and smart, but being a pirate and carrying on a family legacy was far beyond anything she ever thought she could do. She did not believe she had the **fortitude**[9] to do it. What if she came upon some **dastardly**[10], **treacherous**[11] pirate who knew that she was a **novice**[12] and would **deride**[13] or **ridicule**[14] her? Worse yet, what if he skewered her through the heart with a sword? Aunt Tessie took her hand and spoke gently to Ashley, trying to **coax**[15] her into believing in herself.

---

[6] brimming (adj) filled to capacity; (s) full, awash; (a) empty

[7] authority (n) the power or right to give orders or make decisions; (s) power, control; (a) student

[8] conscientious (adj) characterized by extreme care and great effort; (s) scrupulous, careful; (a) lazy

[9] fortitude (n) strength of mind that enables one to endure adversity; (s) courage, bravery; (a) fear

[10] dastardly (adj) extremely wicked; (s) ignoble, shameful; (a) brave

[11] treacherous (adj) dangerously unstable and unpredictable; (s) dishonest, false; (a) safe

[12] novice (n) someone new to a field or activity; (s) beginner, rookie; (a) pro

[13] deride (v) treat or speak of with contempt; (s) ridicule, mock; (a) praise

[14] ridicule (v) language or behavior intended to mock or humiliate; (s) taunt, scorn; (a) respect

[15] coax (v) influence or urge by gentle urging, caressing, or flattering;(s) persuade, urge; (a) argue

"Don't be **dismayed**[16], child. You'll be fine. It's in your blood." It was clear that Aunt Tessie spent many years honing her powers of **persuasion**[17] as she tried to put Ashley at ease. "It will be your first real pirate adventure. But be forewarned, you are never to speak of this to anyone outside of the pirate circle and, if asked, you are to **disavow**[18] any knowledge of pirates."

"Can Ben help me?"

"You have someone else who will be helping you. He is also sworn to secrecy, just like you, and will be a fine **asset**[19] in helping you find the treasure." Aunt Tessie had such an even **temperament**[20] - it really helped Ashley to be confident. She was a loving woman with grace, **poise**[21] and charm, even at one hundred and two.

"But, what about Ben? I can't tell him anything about this?"

"I'm afraid not. This secret is only for you, at least in this family."

---

[16] dismayed (adj) struck with fear, dread, or consternation; (s) shocked, alarmed; (a) delighted

[17] persuasion (n) communication intended to induce belief or action; (s) conviction, belief; (a) force

[18] disavow (v) refuse to acknowledge; (s) deny, repudiate; (a) agree

[19] asset (n) a useful or valuable quality; (s) benefit, advantage; (a) liability

[20] temperament (n) your usual mood; (s) nature, character; (a) rage

[21] poise (n) great coolness and composure under strain; (s) composure, aplomb; (a) insanity

"Hmm. What about mom?"

"Your mother wasn't interested in becoming pirate or being a part of her family legacy. That's why you were chosen instead. Do you accept the challenge?"

Nothing in the world could **dissuade**[22] Ashley from finding out more about her family and becoming a pirate.

Ashley smiled a crooked smile. "The pirate, Ashley Bonny. It has a ring to it."

"Frankly, I think Ash Bonny is a better pirate name. It embodies and **accentuates**[23] the spirit of piracy."

"Oh yes! Ash Bonny."

"Now remember, even if you feel like giving up during the quest, you must **persevere**[24]. You only get one chance to prove yourself."

"One chance? That's it?"

"Only one. Give me your **pledge**[25] that no matter what you will finish."

---

[22] dissuade (v) turn away from by persuasion; (s) deter, divert; (a) impel

[23] accentuate (v) stress or single out as important; (s) stress, emphasize; (a) diminish

[24] persevere (v) be persistent, refuse to stop; (s) persist, continue; (a) quit

[25] pledge (v) promise solemnly and formally; (s) promise, vow; (a) disobey

"I swear I won't give up."

"Then by **decree**[26], you are now officially a pirate in training. Shall we play some cards? Would you prefer Go Fish or War?"

Anything else in the world except pirates was **immaterial**[27] at this moment. Ashley had an **abundant**[28] amount of energy and only one thing on her mind - pirates!

"Can we read your book instead?"

"The reading of that **epic**[29] tale will have to wait, but trust me, the **saga**[30] you will read will be well worth it. You will read of how I found my treasure and then one day you will write a story of you own. You simply must follow the clues to find your treasure, but that can't begin until after school tomorrow."

"Tomorrow?" Ashley shouted. "Why can't we start now?"

---

[26] decree (n) a legally binding command or decision; (s) order,command; (a) plea

[27] immaterial (adj) lacking importance; not mattering one way or the other; (s) trivial, ethereal; (a) real

[28] abundant (adj) present in great quantity; (s) plentiful, copious; (a) lacking

[29] epic (n) a long narrative poem telling of a hero's deeds; (s) legend, heroic; (a) little

[30] saga (n) a narrative telling the adventures of a hero or a family; (s) story, legend; (a) biography

"Don't **fret**[31], child. You are on the **fringe**[32] of something quite incredible. Now, *we* cannot start because it's not my hunt, it's yours. I know where the treasure is and I'm not going to help you. You must do this on your own - with a little help."

Ashley pouted and ran her hand through the treasure inside the chest. Aunt Tessie yawned.

"Actually, I'm feeling a bit of **fatigue**[33]. Why don't we call it a night?"

As disappointed as Ashley was with spending so little time with Aunt Tessie, she made a **feeble**[34] attempt at looking tired and agreed. She felt a little **exasperation**[35] at being made to go to bed and couldn't wait for tomorrow to come. They left the attic and went to the room where Ashley always slept. It was on the second floor and everything in the room was blue and white stripes, Ashley's favorite. It wasn't until she walked in the room that night that she realized the whole room was in a **nautical**[36] theme, almost

---

[31] fret (v) worry unnecessarily or excessively; (s) worry, irritate; (a) calm

[32] fringe (n) the outside boundary or surface of something; (s) verge, edge; (a) middle

[33] fatigue (n) temporary loss of strength and energy from hard work; (s) tire, weary; (a) energize

[34] feeble (adj) pathetically lacking in force or effectiveness; (s) weak, frail; (a) strong

[35] exasperation (n) actions that cause great irritation; (s) rage, irritation; (a) comfort

[36] nautical (adj) relating to or involving ships or shipping or navigation or seamen; (s) marine, oceanic; (a) terrestrial

to **foreshadow**[37] this very night. There were bits and pieces of boats hanging on the walls, sailor's rope tied back the curtains, and there was pirate ship in a bottle on the far table. She picked up the ship in a bottle and began to **reminisce**[38] about the first time she played with it. Spending so many nights here, she should have had the **foresight**[39] to see that there was a secret hidden amongst it all.

"Now it all makes sense," she said as she turned back to Tessie. Aunt Tessie smiled and kissed Ashley's forehead with love and **compassion**[40]. She put a hand to the young girl's cheek and looked her in the eyes.

"You will make a fine pirate," she said. "Now off to sleep with you. You have much work to do."

---

[37] foreshadow (v) indicate by signs; (s) bode, portend; (a) past
[38] reminisce (v) recall the past; (s) recall, remember; (a) forget
[39] foresight (n) seeing ahead; knowing in advance; foreseeing; (s) presage, portent; (a) hindsight
[40] compassion (n) a deep awareness of and sympathy for another's suffering; (s) mercy, kindness; (a) cruelty

Chapter 6

In the **solitude**[1] of the bedroom, she could not keep her mind from wandering. Even through her extreme **weariness**[2], falling asleep was quite a **feat**[3]. When she finally did sleep, Ashley's dreams were filled with **ferocious**[4] pirates and sailing ships, and she was on deck as their **accomplice**.[5] They were making their way across the high seas, sails unfurled and a pirate flag waving from the highest mast. There course was **aimless**[6], but not their purpose. Cannons rumbled and men shouted "Ahoy!" as they drank rum and waved their swords. She was too young to drink and was hoping that wasn't a requirement for being a pirate. Her dreams were fanciful, mimicking the pirate tales that she had seen in the movies.

When she woke, it was a **sublime**[7] morning. She lay in bed for a moment, wondering if it was truly **plausible**[8] that she really was related to pirates and today she would find a treasure. Even the

---

[1] solitude (n) a state of social isolation; (s) isolation, privacy; (a) company

[2] weariness (n) temporary loss of strength and energy from hard work; (s) fatigue, tiredness; (a) energy

[3] feat (n) a notable achievement; (s) deed, act; (a) defeat

[4] ferocious (adj) marked by extreme and violent energy; (s) savage, wild; (a) calm

[5] accomplice (n) a person who joins with another in carrying out some plan; (s) ally, partner; (a) foe

[6] aimless (adj) without aim or purpose; (s) wandering, pointless; (a) directed

[7] sublime (adj) inspiring awe; (s) superb, grand; (a) lowly

[8] plausible (adj) apparently reasonable and valid, and truthful; (s) possible, likely; (a) unlikely

thought of this made her realize that the **normalcy**[9] of her life was gone. After last night, everything was going to change. Soon, she would no longer be a mere **mortal**[10], **frivolous**[11] with thoughts and dreams, but an honest to goodness pirate. She never thought she would feel this kind of **sentiment**[12] for pirates, but knowing that this was her heritage gave her a burning **desire**[13] to become one herself. All she had to do is survive the **onerous**[14] task of finding the treasure.

Ashley was an eternal **optimist**[15] and knew that the day would be filled with excitement. She brushed her teeth and hurried down the stairs for breakfast. She had a **voracious**[16] appetite and Aunt Tessie was waiting at the table for her with pancakes.

"Pancakes!" Ashley shouted as her hand reached for the bottle of syrup. "They look absolutely **delectable**[17]," she squealed as a

---

[9] normalcy (n) the state of being within the range of regular functioning; (s) normal, balance; (a) anomaly

[10] mortal (n) subject to death; (s) human, person; (a) immortal

[11] frivolous (adj) not serious in content or attitude or behavior; (s) silly, foolish; (a) serious

[12] sentiment (n) a personal belief or judgment; (s) feeling, opinion; (a) contempt

[13] desire (n) the feeling that accompanies an unsatisfied state; (s) wish, want; (a) dislike

[14] onerous (adj) burdensome; (s) hard, difficult; (a) easy

[15] optimist (n) a person disposed to take a favorable view of things; (s) dreamer, hopeful; (a) realist

[16] voracious (adj) devouring or craving food in great quantities; (s) greedy, piggish (a) quenched

[17] delectable (adj) extremely pleasing to the sense of taste; (s) tasty, yummy; (a) bad

deluge[18] of syrup ran down the side of the stack. No matter how excited she was, she never would have **deprived**[19] herself of Aunt Tessie's homemade pancakes. They weren't anywhere close to being like those **despicable**[20] ones you buy at a fast food restaurant. They were heavenly!

"I figured you needed your energy. Now eat up so you aren't late for school."

Ashley would never **defy**[21] her Aunt Tessie and ate faster than she had ever eaten before. She rinsed her plate and put it into the dishwasher. For the first time, Ashley was excited about leaving Aunt Tessie's house but, as always, she was excited about coming back too so that she could tell Tess Bonny all about her treasure hunt.

Aunt Tessie, in her most lovely, **melodious**[22] voice, said,"It's time to go." She put a gentle hand on Ashley's back, trying to **assuage**[23] her anxious state, and escorted her to the front door.

---

[18] deluge (n) an overwhelming number or amount; (s) swamp, flood; (a) drought

[19] deprived (adj) marked by deprivation especially of the necessities of life or healthful environmental influences; (s) needy, denied; (a) wealthy

[20] despicable (adj) morally reprehensible; (s) vile, mean; (a) noble

[21] defy (v) resist or confront with resistance; (s) resist, challenge; (a) obey

[22] melodious (adj) having a musical sound; especially a pleasing tune; (s) musical, melodic; (a) harsh

[23] assuage (v) cause to be more favorably inclined; (s) soothe, allay; (a) upset

There, Aunt Tessie gave her a special bag filled with surprises for Ashley to take with her. Ashley went to peek inside the bag, but Aunt Tessie stopped her.

"You're late, child. You can look at it when you get to school. Now, off with you! **Scurry**[24]!"

"But…"

Ashely wanted to know what was inside the bag.

"And don't **deviate**[25] from your task. You can have your look once you get to school, but no peeking until it's time. We may be pirates, but we have **integrity**[26]. Promise?"

Ashley huffed.

"I promise."

Aunt Tessie kissed Ashley goodbye and shooed her out the door. Ashley grabbed a rubber band to **tame**[27] her usually **unkept**[28] hair and pulled it **taut**[29] atop her head. In sheer **jubilation**[30], she jumped on her bike and peddled so fast to school that she began to

---

[24] scurry (v) move about or proceed hurriedly; (s) rush, scamper; (a) dawdle

[25] deviate (v) turn aside; turn away from; (s) diverge, stray; (a) keep

[26] integrity (n) moral soundness; (s) honesty, uprightness; (a) deception

[27] tame (v) correct by punishment or discipline; (s) train, subdue; (a) wild

[28] unkept (adj) having been violated or disregarded; (s) rugged, disordered; (a) kept

[29] taut (adj) pulled or drawn tight; (s) tense, tight; (a) loose

[30] jubilation (n) a feeling of extreme joy; (s) glee, happiness; (a) sorrow

perspire[31]. The excitement of high school seemed dwarfed by the real-life adventure she was about to undertake this afternoon. She was in pure **bliss**[32] knowing that she had a special secret. As she peddled along, so many thoughts crossed her mind.

I wonder how big the treasure chest is? Will I be able to carry it? How much gold is inside? Will we be rich? I bet there are diamonds and rubies and emeralds and lots of gold.

The grass in the front yards she passed had **vapor**[33] rising from them as the sun glistened and evaporated off the wet blades of grass. Ashley was peddling at an **unparalleled**[34] speed (for her), but she was having some trouble concentrating and not keeping an eye on the **peripheral**[35] area. It was almost comical that didn't see Mr. Hendrickson's **outlandish**[36] oversized car coming right at her, especially considering that its enormous **chassis**[37] **dominated**[38] the

---

[31] perspire (v) excrete perspiration through the pores in the skin; (s) sweat, exude; (a) dry

[32] bliss (adj) a state of extreme happiness; (s) joy, delight; (a) agony

[33] vapor (n) a visible suspension in the air of particles of some substance; (s) steam, haze; (a) dryness

[34] unparalleled (adj) radically distinctive and without equal; (s) unique, unmatched; (a) inferior

[35] peripheral (adj) on or near an edge or constituting an outer boundary; (s) outer, minor; (a) central

[36] outlandish (adj) conspicuously or grossly unconventional or unusual; (s) strange, bizarre; (a) normal

[37] chassis (n) the skeleton of a motor vehicle; (s) body, framework; (a) core

[38] dominated (adj) controlled or ruled by superior authority or power; (s) ruled, reigned; (a) shared

entire road. She veered to the side just in time to miss being hit and almost ran over the **dour**[39] and **headstrong**[40] Timmy Smith, who was walking defiantly down the side of the road instead of using the sidewalk as he was supposed to. She scraped him slightly with her bike handle, but it was only a **superficial**[41] wound.

"Hey!" Timmy yelled.

Beeeeeeep!!

"Yield! The sign says yield! You didn't yield, Ashley!" Mr. Hendrickson started his **harangue**[42] in a squeaky, **brash**[43] voice. "You almost ended up as a hood ornament!" Mr. Hendrickson was **livid**[44], but this was not a unique occurrence.

"Sorry Mr. Hendrickson," she yelled as she peddled past his shiny old purple Cadillac, happy to have avoided a **catastrophe**[45]. Mr. Hendrickson was known to be considerably **eccentric**[46] and

---

[39] dour (adj) harshly uninviting or formidable in manner or appearance; (s) grim, sullen; (a) cheery

[40] headstrong (adj) habitually disposed to disobedience and opposition; (s) stubborn, willful; (a) calm

[41] superficial (adj) of, affecting, or being on or near the surface; (s) cursory, shallow; (a) deep

[42] harangue (n) a loud bombastic declamation expressed with strong emotion; (s) rant, tirade; (a) tribute

[43] brash (adj) offensively bold; (s) brazen, cheeky; (a) shy

[44] livid (adj) furiously angry; (s) mad, furious; (a) calm

[45] catastrophe (n) an event resulting in great loss and misfortune; (s) disaster, calamity; (a) blessing

[46] eccentric (adj) conspicuously or grossly unconventional or unusual; (s) odd, strange; (a) normal

also for his **erratic**[47] driving. He would sometimes be caught driving on the wrong side of the road, just like he was today, which is why his **acerbic**[48] tone left Ashley feeling a bit peeved.

She pulled into an **alcove**[49] in the school parking lot, weaving between the rows and rows of cars, parked her bike near the gym (since gym was her first class), and ran right past all of her friends without saying a word. Normally, she would be **sociable**[50], but not today. Today she had a purpose. Emma, her best friend, found this a bit **irksome**[51] since she sent multiple text messages to Ashley last night, none of which were returned. She didn't want to **taint**[52] their friendship by not returning the messages, but she was so focused on finishing the day so she could start her treasure hunt. She was frustrated that she couldn't tell Emma about it anyway.

She ran into the gym where she would normally **deplore**[53] the morning ritual of running around the track (hating it so much it was almost **obscene**[54]). Suiting up for it would usually send her

---

[47] erratic (adj) liable to sudden unpredictable change; (s) irregular, fickle; (a) regular

[48] acerbic (adj) harsh or corrosive in tone; (s) bitter, sharp; (a) sweet

[49] alcove (n) a small recess opening off a larger room; (s) niche, recess; (no antonyms)

[50] sociable (adj) inclined to or conducive to companionship with others; (s) friendly, genial; (a) aloof

[51] irksome (adj) tedious or irritating; (s) annoying, irritating; (a) fun

[52] taint (n) the state of being contaminated; (s) stain, poison; (a) purify

[53] deplore (v) express strong disapproval of; (s) regret, lament; (a) approve

[54] obscene (n) offensive to the mind; (s) dirty, gross; (a) decent

into a deep **depression**[55], but today she was excited that this was her **precursor**[56] warmup for whatever battles lay ahead of her today. After getting into her workout clothes, she hit the track and ran the **mandatory**[57] entire quarter mile even before Mrs. Brody started class. She was so excited abut finishing school that she managed to **accelerate**[58] past the first turn faster than she had ever done before, and finish the quarter mile in record time. Mrs. Brody was at the finish line clapping wildly. Mrs. Brody was a **dynamic**[59] woman who had always been a bit **lukewarm**[60] with Ashley, but was now rather interested in her and even offering her an **accolade**[61] for her performance.

"Well," said Mrs. Brody. "It looks as though we have an eager beaver here. I hope you'll be trying out for the track team."

Ashley had never thought about being in team sports before, but today she discovered that she did like to run and put the thought of trying out for the team on her list of things to do.

---

[55] depression (n) sad feelings of gloom and inadequacy; (s) misery, gloom; (a) cheer

[56] precursor (n) something indicating the approach of something or someone; (s) predecessor; (a) heir

[57] mandatory (adj) required by rule; (s) compulsory, required; (a) optional

[58] accelerate (v) move faster; (s) speed up, quicken; (a) brake

[59] dynamic (adj) characterized by action or forcefulness of personality; (s) vital, lively; (a) dull

[60] lukewarm (adj) moderately warm; (s) indifferent, cool; (a) excited

[61] accolade (n) a tangible symbol signifying approval or distinction; (s) praise; award; (a) insult

Once class was finished, she changed her clothes and ran to her next class - History with Mr. Brimton. She really liked Mr. Brimton because he was a **compassionate**[62] and **affable**[63] man with a prominent German **accent**[64] and a quick **wit**[65]. He looked almost like a cartoon, with his head disproportionately larger than the rest of his body, a prominent nose protruding from the center of his face, puffy lips, and his grand ears wiggled when he talked. He was fun to watch and listen to. He knew so much about so many different things and garnered great **acclaim**[66] from scholars who were familiar with history. He was a school icon and the **epitome**[67] of the perfect teacher.

Ashley hoped that he just might bring up something about the history of pirates, so she listened very carefully to every word he said. By the end of class he hadn't spoken about pirates, but talked

---

[62] compassionate (adj) showing or having sympathy for another's suffering; (s) kind, tender; (a) cruel

[63] affable (adj) diffusing warmth and friendliness; (s) friendly, kindly; (a) grouchy

[64] accent (n) distinctive manner of oral expression; (s) dialect, brogue; (a) written statement

[65] wit (v) a man of genius, fancy or humor; (s) humor, cleverness; (a) silliness

[66] acclaim (n) enthusiastic approval; (s) praise, applause; (a) disapproval

[67] epitome (n) a standard or typical example; (s) embodiment, model; (a) antithesis

about **Pueblo**[68] Indians, Ancient Egypt and all of the gods they worshiped. That was interesting.

Her next class was English with Miss Fromm. Her teacher was an **astute**[69] woman with a soft voice and a **chronic**[70] cough, who was very difficult to hear even with the best **acoustics**[71], so Ashley moved her desk to the front of the room to make sure to catch every word. Ashley loved Miss Fromm because she was very **methodical**[72] in her teaching style and super easy to follow, although most of the other students thought she was **bland**[73] and **vapid**[74]. Ashley thought it was important to listen carefully in case she learned about a word or phrase that might be in Aunt Tessie's book that she didn't know. Miss Fromm spoke about the history of the English language, especially the Nordic languages, and Ashley was surprised to find that English wasn't the first language spoken. She just assumed it was because so many people speak it. This was

[68] Pueblo (n) a member of any of about two dozen Native American peoples called `Pueblos' by the Spanish because they live in pueblos (villages built of adobe and rock); (s) town, community; (a) wilderness

[69] astute (adj) marked by practical hardheaded intelligence; (s) clever, sharp; (a) stupid

[70] chronic (adj) long-lasting or characterized by long suffering; (s) constant, persistent; (a) temporary

[71] acoustics (n) the study of the physical properties of sound; (s) sonic, noise; (a) visuals

[72] methodical (adj) characterized by orderliness; (s) systematic, orderly; (a) chaotic

[73] bland (adj) lacking stimulating characteristics; uninteresting; (s) dull, boring; (a) sharp

[74] vapid (adj) lacking significance or liveliness or spirit or zest; (s) dull, uninteresting; (a) lively

good to know in case she came upon another language in the pirate book or on her adventure, she wouldn't be thrown off of her task.

The bell rang and it was time for lunch. She ran from class with all the **vivacity**[75] of a young colt. Normally, Ashley would hang out with her friends, eating her lunch in the middle of the school yard close to the baseball field, but today she wanted to find a **quiescent**[76] place to be alone, maybe under a shady tree, to see what Aunt Tessie had put inside the special bag. She felt it was time to begin the **rudimentary**[77] task of figuring out how to look for her treasure. She knew of a quiet and **tranquil**[78] place to go. There was a large and lovely weeping willow that was at the edge of the school yard down by the creek. It would be the perfect spot to offer her **ample**[79] privacy to collect her thoughts and eat.

She walked down the long field beside the school and down to the path that ran next to the creek. The walk was so much longer than usual - at least it seemed so to Ashley. Coming up to the tree, she was stopped in her tracks. Much to Ashley's **chagrin**[80], there,

---

[75] vivacity (n) characterized by high spirits and animation; (s) verve, spirit; (a) laziness

[76] quiescent (adj) being quiet or still or inactive; (s) quiet, still; (a) busy

[77] rudimentary (adj) being in the earliest stages of development; (s) basic, initial; (a) complex

[78] tranquil (adj) quiet; calm; undisturbed; (s) peaceful, placid; (a) noisy

[79] ample (adj) affording an abundant supply; (s) large, abundant; (a) limited

[80] chagrin (n) strong feelings of embarrassment; (s) shame, embarrass; (a) delight

under the tree, in the very spot which she had chosen to eat her lunch, was a **contemplative**[81] boy, reading **sedentary**[82] against the tree. His slender body was sitting on the ground, knees raised and a jean jacket underneath him to protect his clothes from any dirt that might try to make its way onto his pants. The round of his back was cozied up against the tree trunk casually, almost as if he owned the very spot upon which he sat. The bangs of his black hair swept down his **tanned**[83] face across his eyes and Ashley could barely see the crystal blue of his eyes reflecting from the white pages of the book he was reading. He was so still and perfect, it was almost as if he were a **mannequin**[84].

Ashley was a bit **wary**[85] of this strange boy and kept her distance. She did not expect to **encounter**[86] anyone else here and she certainly didn't want to **encroach**[87] on anyone else who was trying to study, but he was compelling and unique and truly

---

[81] contemplative (adj) deeply or seriously thoughtful; (s) pensive, reflective; (a) silly

[82] sedentary (v) requiring sitting or little activity; (s) inactive, fixed; (a) mobile

[83] tanned (adj) (of skin) having a tan color from exposure to the sun; (s) bronzed, brown; (a) pale

[84] mannequin (n) a life-size dummy used to display clothes; (s) model, dummy; (a) original

[85] wary (adj) marked by keen caution and watchful prudence; (s) cautious, careful; (a) reckless

[86] encounter (v) come together; (s) meet, find; (a) avoid

[87] encroach (v) advance beyond the usual limit; (s) infringe, trespass; (a) avoid

beautiful. No matter how cute he was, she did not want to **violate**[88] his privacy and it only took her a **fleeting**[89] moment to realize that she could not be **complacent**[90] about sharing this space with him. She would **err**[91] on the side of caution, find another place to eat her lunch, and **conceive**[92] a strategy for the afternoon treasure hunt. She tried to convince herself to leave, but there was something about this boy that Ashley couldn't shake. She simply stood there looking at him, lost in a **void**[93] of wonder. He looked up from his book and smiled.

"Hello Ashley."

---

[88] violate (v) to disturb; to interrupt; (s) infringe, break; (a) obey

[89] fleeting (adj) lasting for a markedly brief time; (s) brief, transient; (a) long

[90] complacent (adj) self-satisfied; (s) smug, conceited; (a) modest

[91] err (v) to deviate from the true course; (s) lapse, wander; (a) correct

[92] conceive (v) have the idea for; (s) create, devise; (a) destroy

[93] void (n) the state of nonexistence; (s) vacant, empty; (a) filled

Chapter 7

Ashley felt her heart stop.

I don't know him. How does he know who I am?

She could not **verify**[1] who this boy was and no one else was in the **vicinity**[2], so she felt extremely **vulnerable**[3]. Her knees grew weak and she felt her legs **warble**[4]. It was as if she took a **bashful**[5] pill because her mind stopped working and she couldn't remember how to speak - so much so that her voice simply wouldn't listen to her brain when it was told to speak. She opened her mouth and all that came out was a very funny sounding "Iiiigggh" that was complete and utter **drivel**[6].

*Well, that was **eloquent**[7], **elegant**[8], and **effective**[9]. Dork!*

---

[1] verify (v) confirm the truth of; (s) check, test; (a) refute

[2] vicinity (n) a surrounding or nearby region; (s) proximity, area; (a) distance

[3] vulnerable (n) capable of being wounded or hurt; (s) exposed, weak; (a) safe

[4] warble (v) to cause to quaver or vibrate; (s) quaver, discant; (a) monotone

[5] bashful (adj) self-consciously timid; (s) shy, timid; (a) confident

[6] drivel (n) a worthless message; (s) nonsense, twaddle; (a) fact

[7] eloquent (adj) expressing yourself readily, clearly, effectively; (s) articulate, fluent; (a) dumb

[8] elegant (adj) refined and tasteful in appearance, behavior, or style; (s) classy, graceful; (a) awkward

[9] effective (adv) producing or capable of producing an intended result; (s) useful, powerful; (a) feeble

What she had meant to say was "Who are you and how do you know who I am?"

The boy was trying to be **jocular**[10] when he said, "Well, that was a **feeble**[11] attempt at the English language. And here I thought the Bonnys were well-**versed**[12] in speaking." He gave a hearty laugh. "Come and sit next to me. We have so much to talk about, if you can manage anything but jumbled words."

The boy was trying to **wheedle**[13] her into joining him and it was a kind **invitation**[14], but it was an awkward **predicament**[15] being in front of a beautiful boy and not being able to speak.

"Who are you?" Ashley asked from a safe distance.

The boy put the book on his lap and asked, "Didn't you read the letter?"

---

[10] jocular (adj) characterized by jokes and good humor; (s) jolly, playful; (a) sad

[11] feeble (adj) pathetically lacking in force or effectiveness; (s) weak, frail; (a) strong

[12] versed (adj) thoroughly acquainted through study or experience; (s) skilled, adept; (a) ignorant

[13] wheedle (v) to entice by soft words; (s) coax, cajole; (a) force

[14] invitation (n) a request to be present or take part in something; (invite,call; (a) farewell

[15] predicament (n) an unpleasant or difficult situation; (s) dilemma, pickle; (a) luck

Now, Ashley was **prone**[16] to being a little forgetful at times and the excitement of the morning certainly caused her head to spin, but she was quite sure that no one had given her a letter.

"Letter? What letter?" Ashley had no idea what this boy was talking about.

The boy laughed an **arrogant**[17] laugh and stood up, putting the book into a small backpack and throwing it over his shoulder.

"You can't be Ash Bonny. Ash Bonny would know what I was talking about."

The boy **strut**[18] over to Ashley and reached into the bag that Aunt Tessie gave her this morning. He pulled out an envelope, **discarded**[19] it onto the ground, shook his head, and walked away. This boy was very **curt**[20] with Ashley and it started to **aggravate**[21] her. At first he was playful and **cordial**[22], but now he was rude and **quarrelsome**[23]? Ashley bent over and picked up the envelope. In

---

[16] prone (adj) having a tendency; (s) inclined, apt; (a) unlikely

[17] arrogant (adj) having or showing feelings of unwarranted importance; (s) proud, cocky; (a) humble

[18] strut (v) walk with a lofty proud gait; (s) swagger, prance; (a) hobble

[19] discarded (adj) thrown away; (s) left, dropped; (a) wanted

[20] curt (adj) marked by rude or peremptory shortness; (s) short, blunt; (a) polite

[21] aggravate (v) exasperate or irritate; (s) irritate, provoke; (a) comfort

[22] cordial (adj) politely warm and friendly; (s) genial, friendly; (a) rude

[23] quarrelsome (adj) given to arguing; (s) belligerent, irritable; (a) peaceful

that instant, she was feeling a bit of **malice**[24] towards this boy. How could he **chastise**[25] her like this? He didn't even know her. She seriously wanted to **pummel**[26] him.

"Where are you going?"she yelled after him.

"You'll never find the treasure if you can't even find the clues. I'll do this **scavenger**[27] hunt alone, thank you!" he said over his shoulder.

She couldn't believe that this boy, whom she didn't know, was being so **brazen**[28]. Was he doing this simply to **antagonize**[29] her?

"Well, I thought this was my lunch and I wasn't hungry yet."

She looked down at the envelope and read the writing on the front:

READ ME WHEN YOU GET TO SCHOOL

Crap!

---

[24] malice (v) to regard with extreme ill will; (s) spite, hatred; (a) kindness
[25] chastise (v) censure severely; (s) punish, scold; (a) pardon
[26] pummel (v) strike, usually with the fist; (s) strike, beat; (a) fail
[27] scavenger (n) someone who collects things discarded by others; (s) searcher, collector; (a) producer
[28] brazen (adj) unrestrained by convention or propriety; (s) bold, cheeky; (a) shy
[29] antagonize (v) provoke the hostility of; (s) clash, annoy; (a) agree

She tore open the envelope and took out the **document**[30] - which was a handwritten, **anonymous**[31] letter - and started to read.

GO TO THE WILLOW TREE BY THE CREEK AFTER SCHOOL AND MEET JOSH ROBERTS, DIRECT DESCENDANT OF THE INFAMOUS PIRATE BARTHOLOMEW ROBERTS. HE IS ALSO EARNING HIS PIRACY STATUS TODAY. YOU MUST WORK TOGETHER TO FIND THE TREASURE.

Great! Here was this **abominable**[32], **pompous**[33] boy that she was stuck working with. There must be an **alternative**[34]. Her anxiety was **augmented**[35] and all she could think of was that working with this boy would be the **equivalent**[36] of going to the dentist and she, like most people, didn't like the dentist. It annoyed her to think that she had no other choice than to work with this

---

[30] document (n) writing that provides information; (s) record, report; (a) speech

[31] anonymous (adj) having no known name or identity or known source; (s) unknown, unidentified; (a) named

[32] abominable (adj) unequivocally detestable; (s) vile, horrible; (a) enjoyable

[33] pompous (adj) puffed up with vanity; (s) arrogant, conceited; (a) modest

[34] alternative (n) one of a number of things from which only one can be chosen; (s) choice, option; (a) duty

[35] augmented (adj) added to or made greater in amount or number or strength; (s) enlarged, raised; (a) less

[36] equivalent (adj) being essentially equal to something; (s) equal, same; (a) different

pithy[37], **temperamental**[38] boy. But she had made a promise to Aunt Tessie that, no matter what, she wouldn't give up.

"Josh, wait!" Ashley yelled as she ran clumsily after him.

He stopped and turned **stoically**[39] back to her.

"Look, I **aspire**[40] to being a pirate and I'm getting my pirate status today. I don't want to be dragged down by some wannabe, **pusillanimous**[41] girl. I'd rather be **autonomous**[42]. We get one chance and I'm not going to **squander**[43] it. I need someone who has the **skill**[44] to take on this task and that's not you."

Josh walked away again.

---

[37] pithy (adj) concise and full of meaning; (s) terse, short; (a) verbose

[38] temperamental (adj) subject to sharply varying moods; (s) volatile, moody; (a) stable

[39] stoically (adv) without emotion; in a stoic manner; (s) calmly, quietly; (a) avidly

[40] aspire (v) have an ambitious plan or a lofty goal; (s) aim, strive; (a) sink

[41] pusillanimous (adj) lacking in courage, strength, and resolution; (s) timid, coward; (a) brave

[42] autonomous (adj) existing as an independent entity; (s) free, separate; (a) dependent

[43] squander (v) spend thoughtlessly; throw away; (s) waste, blow; (a) save

[44] skill (n) an ability that has been acquired by training; (s) ability, talent; (a) ignorance

"Wannabe? Poo silly whatever you said? Stop speaking to me in that weird **jargon**[45]! I'll have you know that I am a direct descendant of one of the most **notorious**[46] pirates who ever lived!"

Ashley was almost **frantic**[47] with this boy's attitude towards her.

Josh stopped and turned to face Ashley. With a **smug**[48] grin on his face, he slowly clapped his hands and gave her a **laconic**[49] response.

"**Kudos**[50]. Me too." And he walked away.

Ashley couldn't understand why he was so **insistent**[51] on leaving and she was becoming very frustrated. She chased after him.

---

[45] jargon (n) technical terminology characteristic of a particular subject; (s) lingo, idiom; (a) formal

[46] notorious (adj) known widely and usually unfavorably; (s) infamous, renowned; (a) unknown

[47] frantic (adj) marked by uncontrolled excitement or emotion; (s) mad, rabid; (a) calm

[48] smug (adj) marked by excessive complacency or self-satisfaction; (s) vain, proud; (a) humble

[49] laconic (adj) brief and to the point; (s) terse, pithy; (a) wordy

[50] kudos (n) an expression of approval and commendation; (s) praise, acclaim; (a) shame

[51] insistent (adj) Insisting; persistent; persevering; (s) stubborn, resolute; (a) tolerant

"Will you stop walking away from me?" Ashley was not someone who liked **adversity**[52] and she was starting to feel a bit of **disdain**[53] for this boy.

"We both have a good pirate **pedigree**[54]. The difference between you and me," he continued while walking, "is that even though I have a fine **lineage**[55] like you, I'm here because of my skill and you're only here because of **nepotism**[56]."

Although her first instinct was to **admonish**[57] him for being so rude, but didn't have much confidence and Ashley questioned whether or not he was right.

"Where are you going?" she said, stumbling along side of him.

He kept walking and gave her a **skeptical**[58] side glance.

---

[52] adversity (n) a state of misfortune or affliction; (s) distress, woe; (a) blessing

[53] disdain (v) lack of respect accompanied by a feeling of intense dislike; (s) scorn, dislike; (a) respect

[54] pedigree (n) the ancestry or lineage of an individual; (s) descent, ancestry; (a) heir

[55] lineage (n) the kinship relation between an individual and progenitors; (s) family, line; (a) origin

[56] nepotism (n) favoritism shown to relatives or friends by those in power; (s) bias, partiality; (a) equity

[57] admonish (v) scold or reprimand; take to task; (s) scold, reprimand; (a) praise

[58] skeptical (adj) marked by or given to doubt; (s) doubtful, disbelieving; (a) naive

"Just because your **kin**[59] are pirates doesn't mean you're automatically a pirate. You have to work at it."

He stopped, snatched the letter out of Ashley's hand, and pointed to two **ambiguous**[60] symbols on the bottom of the letter.

"These are clues as to where we need to go next. Do you know what they are?"

Ashley looked at the symbols on the page. One of them she knew right away, but she didn't recognize the other. It was an odd, **abstract**[61] symbol that she had never seen before.

"This is the logo for the bookstore downtown. I don't know the other one."

Josh laughed.

"That's the symbol for Blackbeard. It's telling us to go to the Hidden Treasures Bookstore and find the book on Blackbeard. That's where we'll get the next clue."

"Wow, you're really good at this," Ashley said with **awe**[62].

---

[59] kin (n) a person related to another or others; (s) family, kindred; (a) unrelated

[60] ambiguous (adj) having more than one possible meaning; (s) vague, unclear; (a) obvious

[61] abstract (n) not representing or imitating external reality or the objects of nature; (s) ideal, conceptual; (a) real

[62] awe (n) an overwhelming feeling of wonder or admiration; (s) respect, esteem; (a) disregard

"Yeah," Josh huffed. "I was hoping you were too, but stop trying to **peddle**[63] yourself off as something you're not." Josh started walking again.

"You don't have to go so fast," she said trying not to fall as she stumbled over the leaves and branches along the path.

"The bookstore closes early on Friday."

"But I have to get back to class," Ashley said desperately. She looked at her iPhone and saw that she was already late. She would be in so much trouble for being **truant**[64].

"Surely, you **jest**[65]?" he laughed and walked faster.

Ashley shook her head and decided he was trying to **mock**[66] her. She straightened her backpack, grabbed his arm to stop him, and faced him squarely.

"No," she said with as much **tact**[67] as she could muster.

---

[63] peddle (v) sell or offer for sale from place to place; (s) vend, trade; (a) buy

[64] truant (adj) absent without permission; (s) absent, missing; (a) eager beaver

[65] jest (n/v) tell a joke; speak humorously; (s) joke, kid; (a) sob

[66] mock (v) treat with contempt; (s) taunt, make fun of; (a) praise

[67] tact (n) consideration in dealing with others; (s) finesse, discretion; (a) rudeness

"You just keep getting better and better," he said wringing his hands through his hair. He put his face close to Ashey's and in a harsh whisper said, "It's Friday. School's only a half day today."

He walked away and Ashley just stood there. Her heart had sunk to her feet. This boy was **incorrigible**[68] and Ashley was starting to get angry, not only at herself for making so many mistakes, but also at Josh for being so mean about it. He was supposed to be a **colleague**[69], not a competitor. No matter how stupid he made her feel, she was determined not to let him **infuriate**[70] her. She became **indignant**[71] instead, taking a deep breath and deciding to confront him.

"Look, I'm very **competent**[72] and I'm not usually this distracted. Don't give up on me!" she yelled. The fire of the pirates began to **permeate**[73] through her blood. She had to correct his **erroneous**[74] opinion of her. Her skills and intelligence were **passable**[75] and she knew it.

---

[68] incorrigible (adj) impervious to correction by punishment; (s) unruly, wicked; (a) shameful

[69] colleague (n) an associate that one works with; (s) ally, partner; (a) foe

[70] infuriate (v) make furious; (s) enrage, anger; (a) calm

[71] indignant (adj) angered at something unjust or wrong; (s) angry, irritated; (a) happy

[72] competent (adj) properly or sufficiently qualified, capable, or efficient; (s) clever, able; (a) inept

[73] permeate (v) spread or diffuse through; (s) pervade, penetrate; (a) drain

[74] erroneous (adj) containing or characterized by error; (s) wrong, false; (a) true

[75] passable (adj) about average; acceptable; (s) fair, adequate; (a) subpar

"What is the old **adage**[76]? Practice what you preach."

Josh stopped again and stood there for a moment. He turned and looked at her.

"What do you mean by that?"

"Figure it out for yourself," she said with a smirk. She had changed her **disposition**[77] to match his and offered him a **paradox**[78] of what he had given her earlier. If nothing else, she was an **assiduous**[79] girl with great determination.

Josh thought for a moment and decided to become a **partisan**[80] pirate in the quest with Ashley.

"Come on," he said with a nod of his head in the direction of the bookstore. Ashley ran to catch up to him and they hurried off down the trail.

---

[76] adage (n) a formal or authoritative proclamation; (s) order, decree; (a) claim

[77] disposition (n) your usual mood; (s) inclination, temperament; (a) dislike

[78] paradox (n) (logic) a statement that contradicts itself; (s) absurdity, enigma; (a) axiom

[79] assiduous (adj) unremitting; persistent; (s) diligent, sedulous; (a) lazy

[80] partisan (n) an ardent and enthusiastic supporter of some person or activity; (s) supporter, follower; (a) opponent

Chapter 8

Ashley looked at her iPhone while trying not to fall as they rushed down the street.

"What about my bike? We can get there faster with it."

"We don't have time to go back to the school and get it. We can take a **detour**[1] through the **vacant**[2] parking lot and then down the back alley behind Denny's Cleaners."

"You know a lot about town, but I've never seen you here before."

Josh gave Ashley a sideways glance.

"I've been around. I noticed you."

Ashley stopped and swallowed hard.

This beautiful boy noticed me and I never noticed him? Maybe he was just being **sycophantic**[3].

"Come on. We don't have time lose. The store closes soon," he said, picking up his pace.

---

[1] detour (n) a deviation from a direct course; (s) bypass, deviation; (a) path

[2] vacant (adj) without an occupant or incumbent; (s) empty, blank; (a) occupied

[3] sycophantic (adj) attempting to win favor by flattery; (s) fawning, servile; (a) naive

Ashley did not know how **resilient**[4] she was. She ran, catching up to him and then passing him by. Although running had always seemed strenuous before, this morning's run around the track inspired her and now appeared to simply be a warm up to race Josh to the bookstore. She wanted to show him that she wasn't dumb or lazy. She was pirate material. She dug deep inside of herself, searching for the **robust**[5] runner she knew was buried somewhere, and began to run faster.

She was a fast runner - far faster than she realized - and more **agile**[6] too. She dodged around bikes and people, cars and trash cans. She had gained a lot of ground before Josh ran up next to her panting like a dog.

"Whoa! You don't have to go so fast," he said trying to keep up and catch his breath at the same time. He was, at best, a **mediocre**[7] runner. And Ashley, at that moment, had no patience for **mediocrity**[8].

---

[4] resilient (adj) recovering readily from adversity, depression, or the like; (s) strong, stable; (a) fragile

[5] robust (adj) sturdy and strong in form, constitution, or construction; (s) powerful, sturdy; (a) weak

[6] agile (adj) moving quickly and lightly; (s) nimble, quick; (a) clumsy

[7] mediocre (adj) moderate to inferior in quality; (s) fair, average; (a) superior

[8] mediocrity (n) the quality of being mediocre; (s) average, subpar; (a) excellent

On a **whim**[9], Ashley went faster. Down the street past the car wash, around the corner and through the alley behind the **rustic**[10] building that housed Denny's Cleaners. She burst out of the alley right next to Andy's Taxidermy where Cameron the **Caribou**[11] stood outside to welcome guests. She hardly broke a sweat and before she knew it, she was standing under the sign for the Hidden Treasures Bookstore. She looked up at the old building, with its giant **buttress**[12] welcoming her in.

Josh had stopped far down the street to catch his breath. He was standing in the road, feeling a bit of **dismay**[13] and **dread**[14] at the cramping his side that would completely **debilitate**[15] him. The **callous**[16] old Mr. Gallagher, who was known as a **desultory**[17] driver, tried to drive around him in his bright blue Oldsmobile. When he couldn't pass, he laid on the horn nearly scaring Josh to death. Josh jumped out of the way, staggered to the sidewalk, and

---

[9] whim (n) a sudden desire; (s) fancy, caprice; (a) plan

[10] rustic (adj) characteristic of the fields or country; (s) agrestic, bucolic; (a) urbanized

[11] caribou (n) arctic deer with large antlers in both sexes; (s) reindeer, deer; (a) wolf

[12] buttress (n) a support usually of stone or brick; supports the wall of a building; (s) support, bolster; (a) weaken

[13] dismay (n) the feeling of despair in the face of obstacles; (s) alarm, fear; (a) joy

[14] dread (v) be afraid or scared of; (s) fear, terror; (a) confidence

[15] debilitate (v) make weak; (s) weaken, sap; (a) energize

[16] callous (adj) emotionally hardened; (s) heartless, insensitive; (a) kind

[17] desultory (adj) marked by lack of definite plan or regularity or purpose; (s) erratic, aimless; (a) steady

started walking towards the bookstore. Ashley tilted her head, gave a smile and a short wave, and went inside.

She had been to this bookstore a hundred times and knew every book on every shelf. It was a **reputable**[18] store with a variety of books and **secluded**[19] places where Ashley would sit and read for hours at a time. Mrs. Pixly was behind the counter, sitting amongst a collection of books that it took her years to **augment**[20]. As always, she was reading some romance novel and looked up as Ashley entered.

"Hello Mrs. Pixly. Lovely day," Ashley said as she passed the **garrulous**[21] woman sitting behind her **hoard**[22] of books. Mrs. Pixly adjusted her glasses as Ashley skipped by.

"Hello Ashley. Back so soon? It is such a fine day, a fine day it is indeed. We have many new books that are ready to be loaned or sold."

---

[18] reputable (adj) held in high esteem and honor; (s) honest, respectable; (a) sordid

[19] secluded (adj) hidden from general view or use; (s) isolated, remote; (a) public

[20] augment (v) enlarge or increase; (s) expand, enhance; (a) reduce

[21] garrulous (adj) full of trivial conversation; (s) chatty, talkative; (a) brief

[22] hoard (n) a secret store of valuables or money; (s) store, stockpile; (a) lack

Mrs. Pixly had a **genuine**[23] love of books and shared it with everyone.

Ashley bounced through the **abyss**[24] of endless aisles, up the stairs and towards the section where there was a vast **array**[25] of pirate memorabilia and lore. There, she had recently seen a copy of *The Tales of Blackbeard* on display next to a poster of the first *Pirates of the Caribbean* movie. She reached the top of the spiral staircase and turned the corner to see the book staring back at her. Biting her lips to keep from squealing with delight, she approached the book and took it off of the display. She opened the first page and there it was - another envelope. She looked around to make sure she wasn't being watched and took out the letter, reading the front:

YOU'VE FOUND ME. DON'T WAIT TO OPEN ME.

Her time spent here at the bookstore proved **fruitful**[26] and Ashley was **jubilant**[27] about finding the first clue! She tore open

---

[23] genuine (adj) not fake or counterfeit; (s) true, real; (a) false
[24] abyss (n) a bottomless gulf or pit; (s) void,chasm; (a) sky
[25] array (n) an impressive display; (s) order, arrangement; (a) disorder
[26] fruitful (adj) productive or conducive to producing in abundance; (s) prolific, rich; (a) barren
[27] jubilant (adj) joyful and proud especially because of triumph or success; (s) joyful, happy; (a) down

the envelope and all that was inside was a feather. It looked very old and it was a **subtle**[28] shade of blue with a red **tinge**[29] to it.

A feather?

She put the book back on the display and turned around, bumping directly into Josh.

"This…is…supposed…to…be…a…team…effort…," he said through struggling breaths.

"Well, I didn't want to be held back by someone who wasn't capable enough to keep up and was slowing me down," Ashley said, beaming with pride that she had beat him. There was no **resentment**[30] in her voice, only a calm **reserve**[31] that that showed how much she was **savoring**[32] this moment.

Josh was forced to **rescind**[33] his earlier opinion that Ashley was unworthy.

"Touché." Josh's breath was starting to come back. "What's the next clue?"

---

[28] subtle (adj) difficult to detect or grasp by the mind or analyze; (s) fine, sly; (a) obvious

[29] tinge (n) a pale or subdued color; (s) tint, shade; (a) pale

[30] resentment (n) a feeling of deep and bitter anger and ill-will; (s) spite, anger; (a) delight

[31] reserve (n) formality and propriety of manner; (s) modesty, restraint; (a) freedom

[32] savoring (v) taking a small amount into the mouth to test its quality; (s) enjoying, relishing; (a) disliking

[33] rescind (v) cancel officially; (s) revoke, cancel; (a) allow

Ashley held up the feather. Josh took it and examined it closely.

"Do you know what it is?" asked Ashley.

Josh shook his head. Ashley pulled out her iPhone and looked up birds with feathers that had a **hue**[34] of blue and red. None of the photos that came up looked like the feather in her hand. Then she remembered something from history class this morning and she did a search for Egyptian Bird Gods. There it was. Ashley smiled. The search on her iPhone resulted in a picture of the **sacred**[35] god she had seen in class earlier in the day. He wore an **elaborate**[36] cape and headdress.

"It's Horus," she said.

"Who's Horus?" asked Josh making a face.

"He's the Egyptian Falcon God. We learned about him this morning."

"I wonder what it means?"

---

[34] hue (n) the quality of a color determined by its dominant wavelength; (s) shade, tint; (a) light

[35] sacred (adj) made or declared or believed to be holy; (s) holy, divine; (a) unholy

[36] elaborate (adj) marked by complexity and richness of detail; (s) intricate, complex; (a) simple

"If my **hypothesis**[37] is correct, it means that our next clue must be at the museum," Ashley said confidently. "Let's go find Horus."

She didn't wait or hesitate; she wasn't about to **jeopardize**[38] earning her pirate status by waiting for this boy and was very **decisive**[39] about what to do next. She was being **spontaneous**[40], and even a bit **haphazard**[41], which was completely unlike Ashley. But she didn't mind because she was in a hurry. She had a treasure to find, no **burden**[42] keeping her from it and no one had to **cajole**[43] her into carrying out the task. She pushed past Josh, bounced back down the spiral staircase and began to **traipse**[44] out the door. Not being a rude child, she turned and said farewell to Mrs. Pixly.

"Goodbye Mrs. Pixly. Have a nice weekend!" she sang as she skipped out the door.

---

[37] hypothesis (n) a proposal intended to explain certain facts or observations; (s) guess, theory; (a) fact

[38] jeopardize (v) pose a threat to; present a danger to; (s) endanger, risk; (a) protect

[39] debilitate (v) make weak; (s) weaken, sap; (a) energize

[40] spontaneous (adj) said or done without having been planned in advance; (s) natural, impulsive; (a) forced

[41] haphazard (adj) dependent upon or characterized by chance; (s) erratic, careless; (a) methodical

[42] burden (n) an onerous or difficult concern; (s) load, weight; (a) relief

[43] cajole (v) Influence or urge by gentle urging, caressing, or flattering; (s) coax, persuade; (a) force

[44] traipse (v) walk or tramp about; (s) march, hike; (a) sprint

Chapter 9

Ashley was feeling very **sanguine**[1] and didn't even wait for Josh to catch up as she made her way towards the museum.

"Hey," he yelled as he caught up to her. "Okay, so I deserved that. But we're supposed to be working together as a team."

Ashley stopped walking and looked at Josh.

"After that **tumultuous**[2] start, you want to be friends? You're not just being **cagey**[3]?"

"I have no **ulterior**[4] motive but friends. It's not like I can **usurp**[5] your pirate position."

He held out his hand and Ashley decided to **capitulate**[6].

---

[1] sanguine (adj) confidently optimistic and cheerful; (s) confident, cheerful; (a) pessimistic

[2] tumultuous (adj) characterized by unrest or disorder or insubordination; (s) turbulent, violent; (a) calm

[3] cagey (adj) showing self-interest and shrewdness in dealing with others; (s) crafty, clever; (a) direct

[4] ulterior (adj) lying beyond what is openly revealed or avowed; (s) hidden, covert; (a) known

[5] usurp (v) seize and take control without authority and possibly with force; (s) assume, seize; (a) resign

[6] capitulate (v) surrender under agreed conditions; (s) yield, cede; (a) fight

"I'll agree, with the **explicit**[7] understanding that you stop being mean and cut all the male **chauvinism**[8]," she said.

"**Pardon**[9] me, but I have no **verbose**[10] explanation about what I did. I wasn't trying to **belittle**[11] you. I was simply following orders as they were **dictated**[12] to me. I shouldn't have made you feel **dejected**[13]."

His demeanor was **diminutive**[14] and Ashley could see the **shame**[15] on his face.

"Following orders? Who would ask you to be so **monstrous**[16] to me?"

---

[7] explicit (adj) precisely and clearly expressed or readily observable; (s) clear, definite; (a) vague

[8] chauvinism (n) fanatical patriotism;(s) jingoism, nationalism; (a) girl power

[9] pardon (v) accept an excuse for; (s) excuse, forgive; (a) blame

[10] verbose (adj) abounding in words; (s) prolix, wordy; (a) brief

[11] belittle (v) express a negative opinion of; (s) disparage, pick at; (a) flatter

[12] dictated (adj) determined or decided upon as by an authority; (s) determined, mandated; (a) asked

[13] dejected (adj) affected or marked by low spirits; (s) sad, unhappy; (a) happy

[14] diminutive (adj) very small; (s) tiny, little; (a) huge

[15] shame (n) a painful feeling of embarrassment or inadequacy; (s) embarrassment; (a) honor

[16] monstrous (adj) shockingly brutal or cruel; (s) atrocious, grievous; (a) benevolent

Ashley was **aghast**[17] thinking that someone would tell Josh to intentionally be mean to her when they were supposed to be working together.

"My Uncle Joe told me to **personify**[18] a real pirate when meeting you, just to give you a taste of what it's like. He was wrong. I'm sorry. Friends?"

"Allies," she said.

From that moment on, they formed an unbreakable **alliance**[19] and off they went to the museum. Ashley was not one to **dwell**[20] on bad things and she was happy again in no time.

Although the town was small, they were progressive and **cultural**[21]. Sunset Valley was is an **amalgamation**[22] of old, new,

---

[17] aghast (adj) struck with fear, dread, or consternation; (s) shocked, appalled; (a) unsurprised

[18] personify (v) represent, as of a character on stage; (s) embody, incarnate; (a) objectify

[19] alliance (n) a connection based on kinship or marriage or common interest; (s) union, partnership; (a) separation

[20] dwell (v) think moodily or anxiously about something; (s) settle, focus; (a) proceed

[21] cultural (adj) relating to the shared knowledge and values of a society; (s) artistic, edifying; (a) bestial

[22] amalgamation (n) the mixing or blending of different elements, races, societies, etc.; (s) mixture, mix; (a) isolation

eclectic, **acquisitiveness**[23], industry, **agriculture**[24], **affluent**[25], and **impoverished**[26]. The blend was a perfect balance for learning and growing. Ashley loved her small town because it never became **lackluster**[27].

The Mayor was a kindly, **ethical**[28] woman who ran the city like a big **corporation**[29]. She was plain, almost **dowdy**[30], but down earth and everyone held her in high **esteem**[31]. Her **contemporary**[32] way of thinking helped the town to grow and prosper through green **incentives**[33] and renewable energy. She was one of the few Mayors who never did anything **adverse**[34], even keeping the small

---

[23] acquisitiveness (n) strong desire to acquire and possess; (s) greed, avarice; (a) generosity

[24] agriculture (n) the practice of cultivating the land or raising stock; (s) farming, tillage; (a) industry

[25] affluent (n) a person who is financially well off; (s) wealthy, rich; (a) poor

[26] impoverished (adj) poor enough to need help from others; (s) poor, needy; (a) rich

[27] lackluster (adj) lacking brilliance or vitality; (s) dull, drab; (a) lively

[28] ethical (adj) conforming to accepted standards of social or professional behavior; (s) moral, honest; (a) sinful

[29] corporation (n) a business firm whose articles of incorporation have been approved in some state; (s) company, firm; (a) isolation

[30] dowdy (n) an awkward, vulgarly dressed, inelegant woman; (s) frumpy, tacky; (a) classy

[31] esteem (n) the condition of being honored; (s) respect, regard; (a) hate

[32] contemporary (adj) characteristic of the present; (s) current, modern; (a) old

[33] incentives (n) a positive motivational influence; (s) motives; stimuli: (a) deterrents

[34] adverse (adj) contrary to your interests or welfare; (s) harmful, negative; (a) helpful

town completely out of debt. She was a **contemplative**[35] woman with high morals and not an ounce of **corruption**[36]. With a mere look, she could **convey**[37] a wide range of emotions and her dedication and **conviction**[38] was beyond **reproach**[39]. She was an excellent Mayor and an admirable **authoritarian**.

There was a stage company that performed plays **primarily**[40] by dramatic playwrights, but every so often a new **parody**[41] or **farce**[42] would pop up and the whole town would turn out to support it. The last time Ashley went to one, the play turned out to be a **dreary**[43] piece about a man and his pet rock. There was a movie theatre that showed films, both new and old. The **evanescence**[44] of the old time record stores rang through the town and the last remaining record shop was replaced with a tech store

[35] contemplative (adj) deeply or seriously thoughtful; (s) pensive reflective; (a) silly

[36] corruption (n) lack of integrity or honesty; (s) depravity, dishonesty; (a) honesty

[37] convey (v) make known; pass on, of information; (s) transmit, transfer; (a) keep

[38] conviction (n) an unshakable belief in something without need for proof or evidence; (s) fact, belief; (a) doubt

[39] reproach (n) a mild rebuke or criticism; (s) blame, reprimand; (a) praise

[40] primarily (adj) for the most part; (s) mainly, principally; (a) lastly

[41] parody (v) make a spoof of or make fun of; (s) mock, mimic; (a) true

[42] farce (n) a comedy characterized by broad satire and improbable situations; (s) joke, parody; (a) play

[43] dreary (adj) lacking in liveliness or charm or surprise; (s) gloomy, dismal; (a) happy

[44] evanescence (n) the act or state of vanishing away; (s) fading vanishing; (a) infinity

that sold gadgets to interest every young person and baffle the elderly.

One of Ashley's favorite places was a lovely museum donated to the city by the **charitable**[45] and **philanthropic**[46] Mr. and Mrs. Hodges. Mr. Hodges was once a well-known anthropologist and Mrs. Hodges was an art dealer. It was a match made in heaven when they met, and with their wealth they established the Hodges Museum of Art and History. It was quite extensive for a small **urban**[47] town museum - a **bastion**[48] of learning - and because the Hodges were well connected, they sometimes had temporary exhibits that many other larger museums would envy. This month it was an Egyptian exhibit and Ashley was sure there would be some kind of **homage**[49] to Horus in there.

They got to the outside of the museum and they could hear that there was an uproar inside. The entrance hall echoed with a **cacophony**[50] of people's voices. Something or someone was

---

[45] charitable (adj) full of love and generosity; (s) kind, benevolent; (a) cruel

[46] philanthropic (adj) generous in assistance to the poor; (s) kind, charitable; (a) greedy

[47] urban (adj) relating to or concerned with a city or densely populated area; (s) city, town; (a) rural

[48] bastion (n) a group that defends a principle; (s) defense, breastwork; (a) defect

[49] homage (n) respect or reverential regard; (s) tribute, praise; (a) disrespect

[50] cacophony (n) loud confusing disagreeable sounds; (s) noise, discord; (a) harmony

causing quite a state of **pandemonium**[51] near the ticket booth. Ashley and Josh squeezed their way to the front of the crowd. There they saw at the ticket desk an **appalling**[52] woman in a **gaudy**[53] pink sequined jacket who was being extremely **flippant**[54] with the **meek**[55] front desk clerk. The poor clerk was being absolutely **decorous**[56] trying to **placate**[57] her. The woman was **hysterical**[58] about losing a contact lens somewhere near the Grand Canyon exhibit and she made the **egregious**[59] request to close the museum until she found it. The people watching the **fiasco**[60] couldn't believe this woman had the **audacity**[61] to ask them to close the museum for her and that she would **berate**[62] the nice

---

[51] pandemonium (n) a state of extreme confusion and disorder; (s) chaos, bedlam; (a) calm

[52] appalling (adj) causing shock, dismay, or horror; (s) scary, dreadful; (a) lovely

[53] gaudy (adj) tastelessly showy; (s) garish, flashy; (a) modest

[54] flippant (adj) inconsiderate; (s) rude, disrespectful; (a) courteous

[55] meek (adj) humble in spirit or manner; (s) submissive, mild; (a) bossy

[56] decorous (adj) characterized by propriety and dignity and good taste in manners and conduct; (s) proper, polite; (a) unsuitable

[57] placate (v) cause to be more favorably inclined; (s) pacify, lenify; (a) enrage

[58] hysterical (adj) marked by excessive or uncontrollable emotion; (s) mad, frenzied; (a) calm

[59] egregious (adj) conspicuously and outrageously bad or reprehensible; (s) gross, awful; (a) slight

[60] fiasco (n) A complete or ridiculous failure; (s) disaster, mess; (a) blessing

[61] audacity (n) aggressive boldness or unmitigated effrontery; (s) boldness, nerve; (a) fear

[62] berate (v) to rate or chide vehemently; (s) scold, rebuke; (a) praise

clerk for not doing so. Closing the museum would greatly **hinder**[63] Ashley's quest and **impede**[64] everyone else's enjoyment of the exhibits. Josh was trying to **stifle**[65] a laugh, and if they weren't in such a hurry Ashley would have also laughed at the **hilarity**[66] of the situation, but time was of the **essence**[67].

"Why don't they simply **evict**[68] this women?" Josh whispered.

"I'm afraid that would only **exacerbate**[69] the situation," replied Ashley.

The **courteous**[70] clerk did his best to **appease**[71] the woman, which was an **arduous**[72] task, but in the end he was able to **inveigle**[73] the woman to leave by saying how lovely her eyes looked without the contact lens. Of course, she was quite flattered and happily for everyone, she left before the agitated mob began to

---

[63] hinder (v) be an obstacle to; (s) impede,obstruct; (a) aid

[64] impede (v) be a hindrance or obstacle to; (s) hinder obstruct; (a) assist

[65] stifle (v) smother or suppress; (s) choke, repress; (a) amplify

[66] hilarity (n) great merriment; (s) mirth, glee; (a) boredom

[67] essence (n) the choicest or most essential or most vital part of some idea or experience; (s) crux, nucleus; (a) secondary idea

[68] evict (v) expel or eject without recourse to legal process; (s) eject, expel; (a) include

[69] exacerbate (v) make worse; (s) aggravate; worsen; (a) improve

[70] courteous (adj) characterized by politeness and gracious good manners; (s) polite, gracious; (a) rude

[71] appease (v) make peace with; (s) soothe, placate; (a) annoy

[72] arduous (adj) difficult to accomplish; (s) difficult, hard; (a) easy

[73] inveigle (v) influence or urge by gentle urging, caressing, or flattering; (s) coax, lure; (a) deter

riot[74] against her. It was very **inventive**[75] of the clerk to play upon her ego, something he must have learned from working daily with many people, but it was clear that he almost felt **remorse**[76] about being the museum **sentry**[77] at that moment. Not being **derelict**[78] in his duties, he continued on with his job as if no **bedlam**[79] had occurred.

Ashley and Josh felt **empathy**[80] for the clerk and patiently waited for their turn to get tickets. Normally there was a **fee**[81] to get in, but Josh and Ashley were excited to find out that admission for students was **gratuitous**[82] on Fridays, and they were waved in with their student I.D.s. Ashley scanned the room to see if she could find a sign pointing the way to the special Egyptian exhibit and found one near the stairs.

---

[74] riot (n) a public act of violence by an unruly mob; (s) uproar, tumult; (a) calm

[75] inventive (adj) marked by independence and creativity in thought or action; (s) clever, smart; (a) banal

[76] remorse (n) a feeling of deep regret, usually for some misdeed; (s) regret, sorrow; (a) joy

[77] sentry (n) a person employed to keep watch for some anticipated event; (s) guard, watch; no antonym

[78] derelict (adj) failing in what duty requires; (s) remiss, neglectful; (a) dependable

[79] bedlam (n) a state of extreme confusion and disorder; (s) chaos, turmoil; (a) peace

[80] empathy (n) understanding and entering into another's feelings; (s) compassion, pity; (a) apathy

[81] fee (n) a fixed charge for a privilege or for professional services; (s) price, pay; (a) cash

[82] gratuitous (adj) without cause; (s) unnecessary, unwarranted; (a) reasonable

"This way," she exclaimed. She bounded up the stairs, attempting to **procure**[83] more clues along the way.

"To the right," said Josh behind her.

It was difficult **abiding**[84] by the rule not to run down the hallways, so they hurried at a very fast walk. They passed a very **engaging**[85] docent who was talking about **prehistoric**[86] art to a large group of very **indifferent**[87] and **unruly**[88] children. Ashley marveled at the **lackluster**[89] look upon the children's faces, their **profane**[90] and **irreverent**[91] behavior, and the **irony**[92] of how she felt about the museum compared to them. They weren't trying to

---

[83] procure (v) get by special effort; (s) obtain, get; (a) lose

[84] abiding (adj) unceasing; (s) enduring, constant; (a) volatile

[85] engaging (adj) attracting or delighting; (s) attractive, charming; (a) boring

[86] prehistoric (adj) belonging to or existing in times before recorded history; (s) old, ancient; (a) new

[87] indifferent (adj) marked by a lack of interest;(s) apathetic, uncaring; (a) interested

[88] unruly (adj) unable to be governed or controlled; (s) wild, disobedient; (a) orderly

[89] lackluster (adj) not having brilliance or vitality; (s) dull, dim; (a) lively

[90] profane (adj) characterized by profanity or cursing (s) sinful, secular; (a) sacred

[91] irreverent (adj) showing lack of due respect or veneration; (s) disrespectful, saucy; (a) devout

[92] irony (n) incongruity between what might be expected and what occurs; (s) wit, scorn; (a) truth

be **malicious**[93] - they were simply being children - **primitive**[94] and unable to comprehend the wonders before them at such a young and **tender**[95] age. She realized that to **juxtapose**[96] two very different viewpoints was the exact purpose of art.

---

[93] malicious (adj) having the nature of threatening evil; (s) spiteful, cruel; (a) kind

[94] primitive (adj) belonging to an early stage of technical development; (s) wild, crude; (a) modern

[95] tender (adj) young and immature; (s) mild, sweet; (a) mature

[96] juxtapose (v) place side by side; (s) compare, contrast; (a) gap

Chapter 10

As they hurried down the hall, they could hear the **cadence**[1] of their shoes echoing on the polished floor. They entered a **palatial**[2] and **grandiose**[3] room at the end of the long main hallway. Ashley was **acutely**[4] aware of everything as she looked around for something that resembled Horus. She had an **innate**[5] sense for defining artistic objects and a **keen**[6] eye for detail. As she stepped out into the center of the room, she saw a **gargantuan**[7] bird-like statue in the far corner.

The statue was very tall and **resplendent**[8] , painted in vibrants colors and accented with gold. The head of the statue looked like a hawk or an eagle, but the body was a strong and sturdy man. An ornate headdress adorned its head, and the feathers on the headdress matched the color and pattern of the feather in Ashley's hand. A long flowing cape trailed behind it and to the side, and the

---

[1] cadence (n) a recurrent rhythmical series; (s) rhythm, beat; no antonyms

[2] palatial (adj) resembling a palace; (s) splendid, grand; (a) small

[3] grandiose (adj) impressive because of unnecessary largeness or magnificence; (s) lofty, grand; (a) tiny

[4] acutely (adv) in an acute manner; (s) intensely, very; (a) mildly

[5] innate (adj) being talented through inherited qualities; (s) inborn, natural; (a) learned

[6] keen (adj) Intense or sharp; (s) eager, acute; (a) dull

[7] gargantuan (adj) of great mass; huge and bulky; (s) enormous, gigantic; (a) little

[8] resplendent (adj) having great beauty; (s) splendid, brilliant; (a) dull

bird head was looking proud across the museum as if it owned the entire room. It was **exactly**[9] what they were looking for.

The statue was so beautiful that Ashley stood looking at it with her mouth gaping wide open. She looked so ridiculous that Josh didn't know whether to stare at her or the statue. Ashley had the **ultimate**[10] dumb look on her face. He laughed at her and smiled at how he was starting to **cultivate**[11] a friendship with this silly girl.

"It's amazing," she finally said.

"Yeah, it's impressive. So what do we do now?" Josh asked.

"I'm not sure." Ashley circled the statue, looking at all of its intricate details. She scratched her head. "I don't see anything out of the ordinary, do you?"

Josh walked around the statue looking for anything that might relate to their treasure hunt.

"No. So, this thing is supposed to be a god?" Josh was making funny faces and ducking under the statue's cape. He spread his arms wide and pretended like he was flying around like a complete **buffoon**[12].

---

[9] exactly (adv) in a precise manner; (s) actually, precisely; (a) partly
[10] ultimate (adj) being the last or concluding element of a series; (s) final, last; (a) first
[11] cultivate (v) foster the growth of; (s) nurture, develop; (a) ignore
[12] buffoon (n) a person who amuses others by ridiculous behavior; (s) clown, jester; (a) nerd

"Look at me. I'm a bird god."

He stumbled and with a little **bungle**[13], he accidentally hit a vase on a pedestal which fell from the platform. Luckily, he had good **tactile**[14] reflexes and grabbed it before it broke on the ground. Josh's face was almost white from being so scared about barely avoiding that **calamity**[15], but then his face flushed with embarrassment as he gently set the vase back on its perch. Ashley rolled her eyes and shook her head.

"Can I be **candid**[16] with you?" she said. "You should really **cease**[17] the antics before you become a **celebrity**[18] for breaking an invaluable artifact."

"Got it," Josh said with a sigh. "So, about the statue..."

"I don't see anything special," said Ashley.

---

[13] bungle (v) make a mess of, destroy or ruin; (s) botch, fumble; (a) succeed

[14] tactile (adj) of or relating to or proceeding from the sense of touch; (s) tactual, tangible; (a) ghostly

[15] calamity (n) an event resulting in great loss and misfortune; (s) disaster, tragedy; (a) blessing

[16] candid (adj) open; frank; ingenuous; outspoken; (s) honest, direct; (a) tricky

[17] cease (v) put an end to a state or an activity; (s) stop, discontinue; (a) continue

[18] celebrity (n) a widely known person; (s) star, renown; (a) obscurity

Ashley smiled as she watched Josh walk around the statue. It was a relief to see Josh not being so serious and she thought that maybe they actually could be **compatible**[19].

"What kind of a god is he?" asked Josh.

Ashley thought for a moment back to her class this morning.

"He's the **celestial**[20] god. The god of the sky. Maybe that's it."

Ashley looked up and started scanning the ceiling for clues. She walked the length of the floor to see the ceiling from different angles and sides. When she walked behind the statue, suddenly the light changed and created an incredible **phenomenon**[21]. The sun was streaming in through a large, oval, multi-colored window, reflecting off the statue, and making a moving **projection**[22] on the ceiling. The **sporadic**[23] sunlight was bouncing here and there, dancing in **simultaneous**[24] rhythm with the music playing over the

---

[19] compatible (adj) able to exist and perform in harmonious combination; (s) fit, like; (a) opposite

[20] celestial (adj) relating to or inhabiting a divine heaven; (s) divine, heavenly; (a) earthly

[21] phenomenon (n) a remarkable development; (s) miracle, marvel; (a) illusion

[22] projection (n) the projection of an image from a film onto a screen; (s) equivalent, equal; (a) conceal

[23] sporadic (adj) recurring in scattered and irregular or unpredictable instances; (s) erratic, irregular; (a) constant

[24] simultaneous (adj) occurring or operating at the same time; (s) coeval, concurrent; (a) divided

museum speakers. Suddenly, the light began to **fluctuate**[25]. The **distortion**[26] made Ashley's head whirl with **instability**[27], throwing off her **equilibrium**[28]. The overwhelming feeling of the room swirling around her was **staggering**[29] and the **vacillation**[30] of the light caused her to have a **bout**[31] of dizziness. A **prickly**[32] sensation went through her hands and she almost fainted. Josh caught her by the armpits and held her up.

"**Chivalry**[33] isn't dead. I've got you," he said as he kept her from falling.

"Thanks. You're my **champion**[34]."

Through her dizziness, Ashley continued to watch the light on the ceiling as it morphed into a large pointing arrow.

---

[25] fluctuate (v) move or sway in a rising and falling or wavelike pattern; (s) vary, waver; (a) stay

[26] distortion (n) a shape resulting from distortion; (s) warp, distorting; (a) clarity

[27] instability (n) a lack of balance or state of disequilibrium; (s) fluctuation, volatility; (a) stability

[28] equilibrium (n) a stable situation in which forces cancel one another; (s) balance, poise; (a) imbalance

[29] staggering (adj) so surprisingly impressive as to stun or overwhelm; (s) surprising, astonishing; (a) dull

[30] vacillation (n) a wavering; (s) fluctuation, vibration; (a) constancy

[31] bout (n) a conflict; (s) encounter, shift; (a) dribble

[32] prickly (adj) very irritable; (s) testy, cranky; (a) calming

[33] chivalry (n) courtesy towards women; (s) virtue, valor; (a) cowardice

[34] champion (n) a person who fights or argues for a cause or on behalf of someone else; (s) hero, defender; (a) loser

"Look," she said staring up at the ceiling. Josh looked up and saw the arrow.

"Wow!" he said as he helped Ashley to her feet. "You okay?"

Ashley nodded and caught her breath.

"It's sending us this way," she said. "Come on."

They went in the direction of the arrow to the next room where there was a special exhibit on Peru that had only been at the museum for a few weeks. The exhibit was extensive with a vast array of cultural artifacts including **crude**[35] tools that had begun to **corrode**[36] with time, real mummies encased in glass and x-ray images of the inside of the mummies. The room was arranged in **chronological**[37] order and had exhibits that spanned hundred of years. There was also a life-sized replica of a very famous tomb that had a whole family of mummies inside. Someone was very **meticulous**[38] about putting together this exhibit and it was impressive.

"I don't know anything about Peru," said Ashley.

---

[35] crude (adj) not carefully or expertly made; (s) unrefined, raw; (a) polished

[36] corrode (v) become destroyed by water, air, or a corrosive such as an acid; (s) erode, gnaw; (a) aid

[37] chronological (adj) relating to or arranged according to temporal order; (s) dated, historic; (a) random

[38] meticulous (adj) marked by extreme care in treatment of details; (s) careful, scrupulous; (a) lazy

"My cousin went to Peru for the summer for a summer exchange program. He learned a lot about their history. He said they had a strange burial ritual where they used to take the flesh off of the bodies before burying them."

"Ew!" exclaimed Ashley.

"Did you know they were the first civilization to turn people into mummies?" Josh was looking at the mummy x-rays.

"I thought it was the Egyptians?" said Ashley.

"Most people have that **misconception**[39], but the Peruvians did it almost two thousand years before the Egyptians. See, look at this plaque."

Josh was pointing to an exhibit showing the **spatial**[40] relation of mummies inside of tombs. The sign on the tomb showed an **exhaustive**[41] timeline of how the Peruvians performed their mummification process.

"That is so amazing," said Ashley.

"It says here that they also used to feed their dead," Josh continued.

---

[39] misconception (n) an incorrect conception; (s) mistake, delusion; (a) grasp

[40] spatial (adj) pertaining to or involving or having the nature of space; (s) room, space; (a) temporal

[41] exhaustive (adj) performed comprehensively and completely; (s) total, complete; (a) facile

"What? That's crazy. Dead people can't eat." Ashley shook her head in disbelief.

"I know, it's kind of **morose**[42] to bring food to dead people, but that's how they would **mourn**[43] for them. They would put food and beer in the tombs with the bodies. Can you imagine if they came back the next day and all the food and beer was gone? The only thing left was candy wrappers on the ground because some **phantom**[44] had invited other ghosts over for a big ol' party." Josh was laughing and walking around the room looking at exhibits when a flash of light glistened from one of the tool cases.

"What was that?" he said going over for a closer look.

The light flashed again.

"I think we've found our next clue," he said.

Ashley walked to the case and stood beside Josh. Inside of the glass box was a giant **exotic**[45] arrowhead and on the arrowhead was a skull and crossbones.

"A bit **surreptitious**[46], but it must be our next clue," he said.

---

[42] morose (adj) showing a brooding ill humor; (s) gloomy, glum; (a) jolly
[43] mourn (v) observe the customs of mourning after the death of a loved one; (s) grieve, weep; (a) exult
[44] phantom (n) A ghostly appearing figure; (s) ghost, specter; (a) alive
[45] exotic (adj) anything of foreign origin; (s) strange, odd; (a) normal
[46] surreptitious (adj) marked by quiet and caution and secrecy; (s) furtive, stealthy; (a) open

"Okay...so...let's see. The last clue was an arrow pointing to this room. Maybe the arrowhead is pointing at the next clue."

Ashley bent over so her face was close to the case and tilted her head in the direction that the arrowhead was pointing. The arrowhead was pointing to an **outlying**[47] area of the room directly at a double-spouted jar with the face of an animal on the front of it.

"It's pointing at this jar." Ashley walked to the jar and examined it. Josh followed and started reading the sign for the exhibit.

"It says the piece was made by the Paracas culture between eight hundred and one hundred BC."

"It must be a leopard. It has spots on its chin," said Ashley.

"The sign says it's a jaguar," said Josh.

"Hmm. A jaguar. Maybe the next clue is at the zoo?"

"For some reason that doesn't sound right. Call it instinct or whatever, but something's telling me there's another clue here somewhere." Josh was pacing the room.

"Well, I believe in you, so we'll go with your instinct. Maybe it's the same type of clue as last time. What's the jaguar looking at?"

---

[47] outlying (adj) relatively far from a center or middle; (s) distant, remote; (a) central

Josh walked around to the side of the jaguar and leaned over to get a different **perspective**[48], trying to **perceive**[49] what the jaguar was looking.

"It's looking into that room at the tall, lighted case," he said pointing.

"Well, let's see what's in it."

Ashley and Josh went the short **trek**[50] into the next room which was filled with gems, jewels, crowns and scepters. In the corner of the room was a knight on a horse, both wearing **ornately**[51] decorated armor. The room glowed with bright lights, and all of the glitter of the jewels and gold made it easy to **sustain**[52] their interest in the room. There were so many **outlandish**[53] things to see and all of them worth a fortune.

"Wow, look at all this gold!"

---

[48] perspective (n) a way of regarding situations or topics etc.; (s) viewpoint, position; (a) hopeless

[49] perceive (v) to become aware of through the senses; (s) sense, discern; (a) miss

[50] trek (v) journey on foot, especially in the mountains; (s) tour, hike; (a) stay

[51] ornately (adv) in an ornate manner; (s) flashy, floridly; (a) awfully

[52] sustain (v) lengthen or extend in duration or space; (s) support, keep; (a) halt

[53] outlandish (adj) conspicuously or grossly unconventional or unusual; (s) strange, bizarre; (a) usual

Josh was walking around the room, dazzled by the luxury surrounding him. There was a guard standing in the corner and cameras all around the top of the room. Josh pulled out his cell phone and started to video the room.

"We **prohibit**[54] the use of video in this room. No photos either," the guard said sternly.

Josh put away his cell phone, got close next to Ashley, and whispered in her ear.

"This has to be our treasure, but how do we get it out of here?"

Ashley shook her head. "There's no way our family would **compromise**[55] our safety and ask us to rob the museum to earn our piracy status."

"Yeah, you're probably right, but it was a fun thought for a moment," Josh laughed.

Although this clue was not entirely **conspicuous**[56], the jaguar jar was looking directly at a large case in the center of the room. Ashley breath was taken away by what was inside. It was a large gold crown. It had a golden bonnet on the inner side surrounded by

---

[54] prohibit (v) To hinder; (s) prevent, forbid; (a) allow
[55] compromise (v) expose or make liable to danger, suspicion, or disrepute; (s) endanger, jeopardize; (a) protect
[56] conspicuous (adj) obvious to the eye or mind; (s) obvious, clear; (a) hidden

a **contour**[57] of gold bands with a **congregation**[58] of diamonds, rubies, sapphires and pearls. On the top was a diamond clustered cross towering atop a blue and gold **ornament**[59]. It was the most beautiful thing she had ever seen in her life.

Josh was reading the sign on one of the displays.

"This room is dedicated to the King of Sweden and these jewels are copies of the Swedish Crown Jewels. They're real gold and diamonds and stuff, but they're copies of the King's jewels. There's got be to millions of dollars worth of treasure here."

The guard in the corner approached the kids.

"That's a copy of the Crown of Eric XIV. Impressive, right?" he said to Ashley.

Ashley had seen the guard before at the museum, long ago when he was the **orator**[60] telling people about the exhibits. He was always **aloof**[61] with Ashley and never spoke directly to her, but not today. Today he was very **forthcoming**[62].

---

[57] contour (n) any spatial attributes; (s) form,figure; (a) base

[58] congregation (n) an assemblage of people or animals or things collected together; (s) crowd, group; (a) few

[59] ornament (n) something used to beautify; (s) decoration, trim; (a) blemish

[60] orator (n) a person who delivers a speech or oration; (s) speaker, lecturer; (a) hearer

[61] aloof (adv) remote in manner; (s) distant, standoffish; (a) friendly

[62] forthcoming (adj) at ease in talking to others; (s) extroverted, outgoing; (a) distant

"I've never seen this much gold in one place before." Ashley was awe struck.

"Yup, that's why I'm here. It would be a great **travesty**[63] if any of it were to go missing. There will be no **collusion**[64] to steal jewels on my watch. It's an invaluable collection and I can't **divulge**[65] too much about its secrets, but being the expert that I am, I can verify its **authenticity**[66]. You kids here for a school trip?" he asked.

"Naw, we're on a treasure hunt. We were hoping we could **acquire**[67] this treasure. This is my **accomplice**[68]," Josh said as he bounded up next to Ashley.

Ashley turned on him quickly, appalled that he had mentioned a quest that they were suppose to **conceal**[69]. Aunt Tessie reiterated that is was of **paramount**[70] importance for the quest to be kept a secret.

---

[63] travesty (v) to translate, imitate or represent, so as to render ridiculous or ludicrous; (s) parody, mockery; (a) actual

[64] collusion (n) agreement on a secret plot; (s) plot, scheme; (a) honesty

[65] divulge (v) to indicate publicly; (s) reveal, disclose; (a) hide

[66] authenticity (n) genuineness; (s) verity, reality; (a) error

[67] acquire (v) come into the possession of something concrete or abstract; (s) obtain, get; (a) lose

[68] accomplice (n) a person who joins with another in carrying out some plan; (s) ally, partner; (a) rival

[69] conceal (v) prevent from being seen or discovered; (s) hide, disguise; (a) expose

[70] paramount (adj) having superior power and influence; (s) foremost, leading; (a) minor

Josh caught on and said, "Just kidding!"

"Yeah, just kidding," Ashley said to **corroborate**[71] the joke.

"Yup, this is one special treasure. One special treasure." The guard stood there with his arms crossed, looking quite proud of his job.

"Excuse me," Ashley said to the guard as she pulled Josh to one side. "Nice job almost blowing it. They were **adamant**[72] about us keeping this a secret."

"Sorry, I got a little carried away looking at all the gold."

"Any ideas about the next clue or are you just going to spend our time here drooling over a treasure you can't have?" Ashley was looking around the room at all the stuff.

"Sorry. I'll get my head back in the game. What was the jaguar looking at again?"

"The crown in the middle of the room."

"Well, maybe it has something to do with the king," Josh said as he walked towards the knight on horseback.

Ashley went back to examine the crown. As she stood in front of the tall glass case, the sunlight came through the skylight and hit

---

[71] corroborate (v) to confirm: (s) verify, affirm; (a) deny
[72] adamant (adj) impervious to pleas, persuasion, requests, reason; (s) rigid, firm; (a) flexible

the cross on the top of the crown. A ray of sunlight reflected off of one of the **translucent**[73] diamonds and directly at the neck of the horse. Ashley's heart leapt and she ran over to where Josh was standing next to the horse and rider. The reflection from the sun was lighting up a spot on the side of the armor that was draped around the horse's neck. In the middle of the spot was the letter "B".

"A Bonny Pirate, are you?" Ashley asked the **imperial**[74] soldier, imagining that at one time he guarded an **impenetrable**[75] fortress, a **deft**[76] swordsman with the **ferocity**[77] of a lion.

"That's Gustavus Adolphus the Great. He was a **sinister**[78] man, best known for kicking butt when there was an **uprising**[79] against him. Nothing like having to fight off a **hostile**[80] takeover, but he won that **revolution**[81]. He had a big victory in the Battle of

---

[73] translucent (adj) transparent; clear; (s) lucid, sheer; (a) opaque

[74] imperial (adj) relating to or associated with an empire; (s) royal, regal; (a) minor

[75] impenetrable (adj) not admitting of passage into or through; (s) tough, unbreakable; (a) passable

[76] deft (adj) skillful in physical movements; especially of the hands; (s) expert, skillful; (a) clumsy

[77] ferocity (n) the property of being aggressive or forceful; (s) fury, fierceness; (a) gentleness

[78] sinister (adj) wicked or dishonorable; (s) evil, menacing; (a) good

[79] uprising (n) a conflict in which one faction tries to wrest control from another; (s) revolt, mutiny (a) ease

[80] hostile (adj) wicked or dishonorable; (s) cold, hateful; (a) kind

[81] revolution (n) the overthrow of a government by those who are governed; (s) turn, revolt; (a) calm

Breitenfeld. That's what the 'B' on the horse's neck stands for. Kind of like an honorary badge." The guard seemed to be knowledgeable about the history of the displays, but he didn't know anything about pirates or their quest. Ashley knew the 'B' meant something more, but she didn't know what.

Ashley was frustrated. She wanted to ask the guard some questions, but his history of being **tepid**[82] with her gave her a feeling of **trepidation**[83], and she wasn't quite sure what to ask anyway.

"We're stuck. What do we do now?" Josh was **indecisive**[84] about what to do next.

"Think," Ashley said to herself.

"We have a crown, a cross, a horse and a king. And now what could this **clandestine**[85] clue mean?" Ashley paced and looked around at all of the items in the room.

"A crown, a cross, a horse, and a king? It sounds like a game of chess," said the guard.

---

[82] tepid (adj) feeling or showing little interest or enthusiasm; (s) cool, indifferent; (a) boiling

[83] trepidation(n) a feeling of alarm or dread; (s) fear, fright; (a) calm

[84] indecisive (adj) characterized by lack of decision and firmness; (s) uncertain, doubtful; (a) certain

[85] clandestine (adj) conducted with or marked by hidden aims or methods; (s) secret, covert; (a) open

Both Josh and Ashley smiled and at the same time said, "The giant chessboard in Ashford Park!"

Ashley laughed. "Since there was not Ashley Park, the Bonny 'B' could only get close with Ashford Park!"

"Well, maybe we should change your name Ashford instead," laughed Josh.

"Very funny. Don't you dare **tout**[86] my nobel name like that!" yelled Ashley over her shoulder as she ran from the room.

"Walk!" the guard bellowed after her.

---

[86] tout (v) show off; (s) boast, promote; (a) belittle

Chapter 11

Aunt Tessie had taught Ashley to play chess when she was very young and she was quite **passionate**[1] about it. In fact, she was hoping to join the Chess Club at the high school, but felt she might be too much of an **extrovert**[2] for some of the other members. But she was **intimately**[3] familiar with the **permanent**[4] giant chess board in the center **expanse**[5] of the park because she had spent **extensive**[6] time learning chess with those large pieces. The first time she played there the pieces were almost bigger than she was. She tried in her mind to picture everything around the board and wondered what the next clue would be. It was **critical**[7] that she and Josh figure this out today and it was getting late.

"Do you know how to play chess?" asked Josh as they hurried along.

---

[1] passionate (adj) having or expressing strong emotions; (s) ardent, fervent; (a) bored

[2] extrovert (n) a person concerned more with practical realities than with inner thoughts and feelings; (s) outgoing, sociable; (a) wallflower

[3] intimately (adv) with great or especially intimate knowledge; (s) fully, closely; (a) distantly

[4] permanent (adj) continuing or enduring without marked change in status or condition or place; (s) stable, lasting; (a) temporary

[5] expansive (adj) friendly and open and willing to talk; (s) broad, large; (a) narrow

[6] extensive (adj) broad in scope or content; (s) wide, large; (a) tiny

[7] critical (adj) characterized by careful evaluation and judgment; (s) severe, serious; (a) trivial

"Yeah, and I'm pretty good too," Ashley said with a proud smile. She wasn't confident doing many things, but chess was something she was very good at.

"I'm not that familiar with chess. Okay, so I'm not familiar at all with chess. I've never played and couldn't tell you anything about it. So I guess this one's on you. Do you have any idea what the clues mean?"

Ashley shook her head.

"It could mean all kinds of things. It'll probably come to me when we get there. I mean, chess is pretty straightforward. You move pieces around the board and try to outsmart your opponent, all to capture the king."

"I don't know. Chess always looked kind of **mundane**[8] to me, but you make it sound so easy and maybe even fun. I can't imagine it's that simple."

"It's not. It can **perplex**[9] you, and takes a lot of thought and strategy, but once you get the hang of it, it is really fun and super competitive. You'd like it. You just have to be **diligent**[10] to learn it."

---

[8] mundane (adj) found in the ordinary course of events; (s) dull, boring; (a) magic
[9] perplex (v) be a mystery or bewildering to; (s) confuse, puzzle; (a) clarify
[10] diligent (adj) characterized by care and perseverance in carrying out tasks; (s) careful, attentive; (a) idle

"Maybe you could **endeavor**[11] to teach me once the quest is over," Josh said shyly.

Ashley almost tripped over her own feet and her face grew hot with embarrassment. She could feel herself blushing. It had been such a fun day so far and she really liked Josh. She hoped that they would stay friends after they found the treasure, but she had been too afraid to say anything. For him to suggest that she teach him chess afterwards was almost as if he knew what she was thinking through **telepathy**[12]. Knowing that he felt the same way sent a feeling of **elation**[13] through Ashley.

"I'd like that," she said with a broad smile.

They walked by the barber shop where the **idiosyncratic**[14] Mr. Jensen was sitting on a bench reading a newspaper. His cat, who had a **penchant**[15] for sleeping and was normally rather **idle**[16] and **elusive**[17], was now wandering in the middle of the sidewalk being

---

[11] endeavor (n) a purposeful or industrious undertaking; (s) effort, strive; (a) ignore

[12] telepathy (n) apparent communication from one mind to another without using sensory perceptions; (s) insight, telepath; (a) miscommunication

[13] elation (n) a feeling of joy and pride; (s) happiness, joy; (a) agony

[14] idiosyncratic (adj) peculiar to the individual; (s) odd, peculiar; (a) normal

[15] penchant (n) a strong liking; (s) inclination, leaning; (a) dislike

[16] idle (adj) not in action or at work; (s) inactive, lazy; (a) busy

[17] elusive (adj) difficult to detect or grasp by the mind or analyze; (s) tricky, evasive; (a) easy

very **insistent**[18] on getting picked up. Ashley stopped to pet her as she meowed at her feet. Although the cat was a bit odd and not very bright, it was sweet and soft, and seeing it started to **evoke**[19] a longing inside of Ashley for a pet. Ashley picked up the cat and Josh gave the cat's head a scratch.

"Do you have any pets?" he asked Ashley.

"No, my mom's allergic to fur. At least, that's what she says. I think she's allergic to cleaning fur."

Josh laughed. "Mine too. I mean, she's not **fanatical**[20] about it, but she doesn't like the shedding fur. No indoor fur she said. So I outsmarted her by getting a rabbit. I keep it in a cage in the backyard. No indoor fur. He's all black and his name is…"

"Blackbeard?" asked Ashley.

"You're good. So, how long have you known about your family being pirates?"

Ashley put down the cat and stormed off.

"What did I say?" asked Josh as he ran after her.

---

[18] insistent (adj) demanding attention; (s) stubborn, relentless; (a) tolerant
[19] evoke (v) call forth; (s) arouse, elicit; (a) halt
[20] fanatical (adj) marked by excessive enthusiasm for and intense devotion to a cause or idea; (s) zealous, rabid; (a) pedant

"It hasn't even been a day. Okay, maybe it's close to twenty-four hours, but barely a day. I honestly can't **fathom**[21] why no one ever told me about this. Fourteen years I could have been studying and working on doing pirates things, but no. My Aunt Tessie didn't trust me with a secret. Me! Her very own great niece. It's simply not **feasible**[22]! She didn't trust me! Grrr!"

Ashley stormed off, stomping her feet and muttering to herself. Josh could see that she was **overwrought**[23] with anxiety.

"Uh, I guess I shouldn't have asked," said Josh timidly as he caught up to her.

Ashley stopped again and faced Josh squarely. "What about you? How long have you known?"

"Uh…ugh…ggggrg…" Is all that came out of Josh.

Ashly looked at him with **contempt**[24].

---

[21] fathom (v) come to understand; (s) penetrate, grasp; (a) interpret

[22] feasible (adj) capable of being done, executed or effected; (s) possible, viable; (a) impossible

[23] overwrought (adj) deeply agitated especially from emotion; (s) distraught, upset; (a) calm

[24] contempt (n) lack of respect accompanied by a feeling of intense dislike; (s) disdain, scorn; (a) respect

"Well, that was a **feeble**[25] attempt at the English language. And here I thought the Roberts Pirates were well-**versed**[26] in speaking."

And she stormed off again. Ashley didn't realize she could be this **overbearing**[27]. Josh chased after her and grabbed her by the arm to **subdue**[28] her.

"What?" she whirled on him.

"Look, each family is different and not telling you was probably just a **faux pas**[29]. I'm sure it was nothing personal... about you...why they didn't tell you. They probably just didn't want you to get in trouble. I mean, it's not like they're telling you we're royalty or something. We're pirates."

"No. My Aunt Tessie told me that she waited until I was old enough to keep a secret. That really hurt. It's **baffling**[30] to think that the one person I cared most about in the entire world didn't trust me until yesterday."

---

[25] feeble (adj) pathetically lacking in force or effectiveness; (s) weak, frail; (a) strong

[26] versed (adj) thoroughly acquainted through study or experience; (s) skilled, adept; (a) ignorant

[27] overbearing (adj) overpowering; subduing; repressing; (s) arrogant, haughty; (a) meek

[28] subdue (v) put down by force or intimidation; (s) suppress, overcome; (a) release

[29] faux pas (n) a false step; (s) mistake, blunder; (a) succeed

[30] baffling (adj) making great mental demands; (s) puzzling, perplexing; (a) easy

Thinking about it made her soul feel **barren**[31] and **bleak**[32], and she couldn't bear the **weight**[33] of knowing that Aunt Tessie didn't trust her. Her face contorted into a **grimace**[34] and she felt a **surge**[35] of tears well up in her eyes. She tried to **suppress**[36] them because she didn't want to **waver**[37] in front of Josh.

"Come here," Josh said kindly.

Josh felt **sympathy**[38] for her **grave**[39] sadness, pulled her close to him and tried to **console**[40] her with a hug. She could feel the **kinetic**[41] energy between them and the closeness made Ashley **wince**[42] as she wiped away a single tear that had begun rolling down her cheek. She took a deep breath, **subdued**[43] her sadness and realized how good he smelled. For a moment, she was

---

[31] barren (adj) providing no shelter or sustenance; (s) empty, bare; (a) full

[32] bleak (adj) offering little or no hope; (s) gloomy, dreary; (a) bright

[33] weight (n) the relative importance granted to something; (s) load, burden; (a) lightness

[34] grimace (v) a contorted facial expression; (s) frown, scowl; (a) smile

[35] surge (n) a sudden forceful flow; (s) rise, rush; (a) ebb

[36] suppress (v) to put down by force or authority; (s) repress, subdue; (a) support

[37] waver (v) be unsure or weak; (s) tremble, sway; (a) decide

[38] sympathy (n) an inclination to support or be loyal to or to agree with an opinion; (s) pity, empathy; (a) apathy

[39] grave (adj) dignified and somber in manner or character and committed to keeping promises; (s) serious, severe; (a) silly

[40] console (v) give moral or emotional strength to; (s) comfort, soothe; (a) disturb

[41] kinetic (adj) characterized by motion; (s) dynamic, active; (a) limp

[42] wince (v) draw back, as with fear or pain; (s) flinch, coil; (a) still

[43] subdued (adj) in a softened tone; (s) quiet, soft; (a) loud

oblivious[44] to anything in the world but Josh. She pulled away from him awkwardly and wiped her nose on her sleeve. Josh wanted to **mitigate**[45] Ashley's sorrow and lifted her chin with his index finger.

"I have four sisters, none of them know and none of them will every know. I was chosen. I understand your frustration."

Josh was looking Ashley square in the eyes, speaking with **axiom**[46] straight from the soul.

"I'm sure it's not true that she didn't trust you. I'm certain that your Great Aunt was simply protecting you. People don't like pirates, but maybe it's up to our generation of pirates to **debunk**[47] all of the myths about them."

Ashley sniffled. "Aunt Tessie doesn't lie."

"Of course she does," Josh laughed. "She's a pirate."

"She's not that kind of a pirate."

"There's no such thing as 'that kind of a pirate'. A pirate is a pirate and once a pirate, always a pirate. Look, you have to understand how hard it is being a pirate these days, especially with

---

[44] oblivious (adj) lacking conscious awareness of; (s) unaware, heedless; (a) aware

[45] mitigate (v) make less severe or harsh; (s) reduce, ease;(a) increase

[46] axiom (adj) a self-evident and necessary truth; (s) fact, dictum; (a) paradox

[47] debunk (v) expose while ridiculing; (s) expose, unmask; (a) conceal

all of the really bad ones giving us a bad name. People look at you as if you're a **felon**[48] whether you do anything wrong or not. Honestly, she loves you and just wanted the best for you. Besides, now you know and you should do everything you can to get your pirate status today and become the world's best Ash Bonny pirate. It's the greatest thing in the world to be descendant from pirates. Own it, enjoy it, become it."

He spoke with such passion and **veracity**[49], but all Ashley could think about in that moment was how adorable Josh was and how his eyes sparkled in the sun. She shifted on her heels and took a deep breath. Her anxiety began to **subside**[50].

"Sorry for being such a **sullen**[51] baby. I just wish I had known a long time ago. It feels like so much wasted time."

"The adventure is just beginning and I've got a **surplus**[52] of hugs. Now come on. Don't let them steal your **zeal**[53]. That's what my dad always says. Let's go find our pirate's booty. I said booty." Josh laughed and Ashley joined in.

---

[48] felon (adj) a person who has committed a felony; (s) criminal, outlaw; (a) police
[49] veracity (n) unwillingness to tell lies; (s) truth, verity; (a) lie
[50] subside (v) wear off or die down; (s) sink, decline; (a) rise
[51] sullen (adj) showing brooding ill humor; (s) gloomy, glum; (a) cheery
[52] surplus (n) a quantity much larger than is needed; (s) extra, plethora;(a) lack
[53] zeal (n) excessive fervor to do something or accomplish some end; (s) passion, spirit; (a) apathy

Josh was **animated**[54] when he was trying to be funny and the **antic**[55] made her **succumb**[56] to his charm. He didn't have a lot of **tact**[57] sometimes, but right now it wasn't needed. In that moment, their friendship had begun to **surpass**[58] her earlier expectations.

"Thanks for making me laugh. You're a good friend."

"Aye matey, I am. Argh!" Josh said in a very bad pirate accent.

---

[54] animated (adj) having life or vigor or spirit; (s) lively, spirited; (a) dead
[55] antic (adj) ludicrously odd; (s) joke, prank; (a) serious
[56] succumb (v) be fatally overwhelmed; (s) yield, surrender; (a) endure
[57] tact (n) consideration in dealing with others and avoiding giving offense; (s) finesse, discretion; (a) rudeness
[58] surpass (v) distinguish oneself; (s) exceed, outdo; (a) lose

Off they went with great **aplomb**[1] and as they walked along, they came upon the bakery. Ashley realized she hadn't eaten since early morning and that would explain why she was so hangry.

"I was hoping I could **muddle**[2] through this without eating, but I'm so hungry. Do you mind if we stop in for a snack?" she asked.

"I'm a fourteen year old boy. I never mind stopping for food."

And the **unanimous**[3] decision was made to eat. They went into the store with great **exuberance**[4] and were instantly inundated with delicious smells. The aroma of fresh bread mixed with sugar and spices permeated throughout the air. The smell was so **enticing**[5] that Ashley could not **withstand**[6] the urge to take one of the samples of the **decadent**[7] peach cobbler that was in a basket on the counter. Sugar was a **vice**[8] of Ashley's - okay, so she was a bit of

---

[1] aplomb (n) assurance of manner or of action; (s) poise, confidence; (a) fear

[2] muddle (v) to think and act in a confused, aimless way; (s) botch, shuffle; (a) adjust

[3] unanimous (adj) in complete agreement; (s) united, agreed; (a) split

[4] exuberance (n) joyful enthusiasm; (s) happiness, liveliness; (a) boredom

[5] enticing (adj) highly attractive and able to arouse hope or desire; (s) alluring, inviting; (a) horrid

[6] withstand (v) resist or confront with resistance; (s) defy, hold out; (a) agree

[7] decadent (adj) marked by excessive self-indulgence and moral decay; (s) evil, wicked; (a) good

[8] vice (n) moral weakness; (s) flaw, defect; (a) virtue

an **addict**[9] - and she could never resist the sweets at the bakery. Ashley's stomach growled as she popped the warm piece of cobbler into her mouth and let it melt on her tongue. Now she was really hungry. She looked over the case of pastries and wanted to eat every single one. In fact, there were few things that contained sugar that Ashley had an **aversion**[10] to and any pastry was **palatable**[11], but it only took Ashley a **minute**[12] to decide which one she wanted to order.

Her friend Elizabeth was working behind the counter. Elizabeth was a gorgeous **debutante**[13] who was somewhat **priggish**[14], but everyone at school knew that one day they would **hail**[15] her as prom queen. All the boys at school were crazy about her. Even with her highbrow status, her parents made her work behind the counter of their store for a **paltry**[16] wage. Everyone thought she was the luckiest person in the world because her parents owned the best bakery in town and while working there she got to eat

---

[9] addict (n) someone who is so ardently devoted to something that it resembles an addiction; (s) nut, freak; (a) oppose

[10] aversion (n) a feeling of intense dislike; (s) hate, distaste; (a) love

[11] palatable (adj) acceptable to the taste or mind; (s) tasty, delicious; (a) foul

[12] minute (n) an indefinitely short time; (s) moment, second; (a) big

[13] debutante (n) a young woman making her debut into society; (s) girl, deb; (a) virtuoso

[14] priggish (adj) exaggeratedly proper; (s) prim, prudish; (a) foul

[15] hail (v) praise vociferously; (s) acclaim, laud; (a) ignore

[16] paltry (adj) Contemptibly small in amount; (s) measly, miserable; (a) big

anything for free. Of course she loved this because Elizabeth was a star volleyball player with a hearty appetite.

Elizabeth was at the other end of the counter chatting away with a cute boy who was trying to **pilfer**[17] a free donut. Now, Ashley usually wouldn't **badger**[18] her friend while she was flirting with a cute boy, but she was really hungry and in a hurry to complete the treasure hunt.

"Hey Elizabeth! We're in kind of a hurry. Do you mind?"

"Hey Ashley." Elizabeth looked at Josh and smiled. "Hi Josh," she said with a slight air of surprise. She looked back and forth between Ashley and Josh. "Do you…two… like…know each other?" It seemed that Elizabeth was a little **covetous**[19] of Ashley and spoke to her in a slightly **belligerent**[20] tone.

"We're best friends," Josh said without hesitation.

Ashley blushed and couldn't help but think of all the rumors that would be started between tonight and Monday morning by Elizabeth, citing her own encounter with them as the **credible**[21]

---

[17] pilfer (v) Make off with belongings of others; (s) pinch, swipe; (a) give
[18] badger (v) annoy persistently; (s) harass, pester; (a) ease
[19] covetous (adj) showing extreme cupidity; painfully desirous of another's advantages; (s) greedy, desirous; (a) selfless
[20] belligerent (adj) characteristic of an enemy or one eager to fight; (s) aggressive, hostile; (a) peaceful
[21] credible (adj) capable of being believed; (s) believable, plausible; (a) incredible

source. Somehow, Ashley didn't care. Having everyone think that Josh was her boyfriend was in no way **daunting**[22] to her. He was amazing.

"May I have a raspberry filled jelly donut and an oatmeal cookie?" Ashley loved the raspberry jelly stuffing because it was made with real raspberries that Elizabeth would hand **mince**[23] and stuff into the dough. Ashley wasn't fond of the fake jelly filled donuts at the store and thought they were **repulsive**[24]. She started to reach in her pocket for money, but Josh stopped her.

"I got this. Make it two of each." He looked at her and smiled.

Elizabeth's eyes grew wide and she was completely speechless. You seem Elizabeth was usually a very **loquacious**[25] girl and it made Ashley laugh to see her unable to utter a word. When she finally spoke it was in a soft quavering voice.

"Uh, sure. Coming right up."

Elizabeth reached into the glass case, took out two jelly donuts and two cookies, and handed them to Josh. He handed them to Ashley and paid Elizabeth.

---

[22] daunting (adj) discouraging through fear; (s) scary, dreadful; (a) agreeable
[23] mince (n) food chopped into small bits; (s) dice, chop; (a) whole
[24] repulsive (adj) offensive to the mind; (s) disgusting, offensive; (a) nice
[25] loquacious (adj) full of trivial conversation; (s) talkative, chatty; (a) quiet

"Keep the change," he said. "Have a great day."

Elizabeth seemed a bit disgruntled that Josh showed no interest in her and only had eyes for Ashley. Josh took Ashley by the hand and they walked out of the bakery. They walked past a few stores before Ashley took back her hand and turned to Josh.

"Well, that was **crafty**[26]," said Ashley.

"What? I may be **thrifty**[27], but I'm not some **petty**[28] **miser**[29]. Why wouldn't I pay for your snack?"

"You know that's not what I meant."

"Oh, you mean holding your hand? Maybe I did it just to **flatter**[30] you. It was also fun to mess with Elizabeth. She looked shocked to see us together, so I thought I'd throw a little fuel on the fire. I hope you didn't find it **distasteful**[31]. Oh crap, you're embarrassed to be seen with me? Or worse yet, you have a boyfriend and I'm going to be the cause of a **domestic**[32] dispute, or

---

[26] crafty (adj) marked by skill in deception; (s) cunning, artful; (a) naive
[27] thrifty (adj) careful and diligent in the use of resources; (s) frugal, sparing; (a) wasteful
[28] petty (adj) small and of little importance; (s) trivial, minor: (a) royal
[29] miser (n) a stingy hoarder of money and possessions; (s) cheapskate, tightwad; (a) spender
[30] flatter (v) praise somewhat dishonestly; (s) compliment, cajole; (a) insult
[31] distasteful (adj) highly offensive; arousing aversion or disgust; (s) repulsive, foul; (a) pleasant
[32] domestic (adj) of or involving the home or family; (s) home, family; (a) outside

worse yet a breakup. I'm so sorry. Just give me his number and I'll call and tell him it was a joke. Ah, I'm such a jerk."

Ashley laughed. "Stop! I don't have a boyfriend and I'm not embarrassed to be seen with you. I actually thought it was funny and sweet. I've never seen Elizabeth shut up like that before." Ashley was laughing and eating her cookie. She handed a cookie to Josh who devoured it in a few bites.

"Good. I didn't think that I might get you in trouble. I was just having a little fun. But…um…I do like you and hope we can stay friends after today."

"I'd like that," Ashley said.

The walk to the park from the bakery was short and the giant chess set was right across the street from the Mini Mart. Luckily, no one was playing on the giant-sized board, but there were a few elderly men with old-fashioned TV trays and folding chairs playing their own game of chess off to the side of the board on the grass. Ashley and Josh crossed the street and walked through the park to the board. They had both finished their snacks and were quite **optimistic**[33] that they were close to finding the treasure.

---

[33] optimistic (adj) expecting the best; (s) hopeful, positive; (a) pessimistic

The pieces on the board were scattered and some were laying on their sides. Josh stood there looking at the board as if he was scared.

"Don't **meander**[34]. Snap to it! We're in a hurry!" Ashley ordered.

Josh went to the piece closest to him and steadied himself to pick it up. The **weight**[35] of the chess piece was **deceptive**[36] and he thought he would have to **strain**[37] to pick it up. He braced himself and yanked hard on the piece. He fell backwards onto his butt and the chess piece went flying over his head. Ashley laughed hysterically and easily picked up the black queen, putting her onto the checkerboard square where she would be at the start of the game. Josh climbed to his feet, dusting off his hands and pants. He was clearly embarrassed. Ashley tried to put him at ease.

"Let's talk about the pieces. Each one is **distinctive**[38]," she said "There are two rooks, two knights, two bishops, and eight pawns for each color. Each person also gets a king and queen. I'll set up

---

[34] meander (n) an aimless amble on a winding course; (s) wander, roam; (a) bolt

[35] weight (n) the relative importance granted to something; (s) load, significance; (a) luxury

[36] deceptive (adj) causing one to believe what is not true or fail to believe what is true; (s) false, misleading; (a) honest

[37] strain (v) to exert much effort or energy; (s) stress, force; (a) rest

[38] distinctive (adj) of a feature that helps to distinguish a person or thing; (s) unique, diverse; (a) normal

the black pieces on this side and you put the white pieces on the other side as a mirror image of the black pieces, exactly the way I'm setting them up here." She tried to keep a steady and **didactic**[39] tone while explaining. "Once they're set up, whoever has the white pieces goes first. You're white so you'd **initiate**[40] the game. It's pretty simple. You don't have to be a super **intellectual**[41] to learn the game."

Ashley didn't want to **inundate**[42] Josh with too much instruction. Keeping it simple would help him like the game, **nurture**[43] his curiosity, and not **mar**[44] any interest he had in learning the game.

"Then how come it's always the nerdy kids that are in the chess club?"

Ashley looked pained. "That was an **asinine**[45] thing to say. I was going to join the chess club."

---

[39] didactic (adj) instructive (especially excessively); (s) preachy, academic; (a) ignorant
[40] initiate (v) bring into being; (s) start, begin; (a) finish
[41] intellectual (n) a person who uses the mind creatively; (s) genius, mental; (a) stupid
[42] inundate (v) fill quickly beyond capacity; (s) flood,swamp; (a) drain
[43] nurture (v) help develop, help grow; (s) foster, nourish; (a) neglect
[44] mar (v) to spoil, to ruin; (s) ruin, damage; (a) improve
[45] asinine (adj) devoid of intelligence; (s) silly, foolish; (a) clever

"Oh, hey, I didn't mean that. You're not nerdy at all. You're...**invigorating**[46]." Josh said, stumbling a bit over his words.

Ashley cocked her head and was a bit **tentative**[47] about asking for clarification.

"Invigorating?" Ashley said with raised eyebrows.

"It's my mom's favorite word. It's a compliment. It means that you make me happy."

Ashley blushed and mumbled "thanks" under her breath.

Josh picked up the castle and asked, "What's the name of this piece?"

"That's a rook," she said. "One goes in each corner of the board. They can move forward, backwards and side to side." Ashley was quite **nimble**[48] when it came to putting pieces on the board and she was done long before Josh.

"There's a whole bunch of these little - well, big little guys. Too bad they're not more **dissimilar**[49]. We could name them."

---

[46] invigorating (adj) imparting strength and vitality; (s) fresh, stimulating; (a) boring

[47] tentative (adj) Unsettled in mind or opinion; (s) timid, uncertain; (a) definite

[48] nimble (adj) moving quickly and lightly; (s) agile, quick; (a) slow

[49] dissimilar (adj) not similar; (s) diverse, different; (a) alike

"Those are pawns. They're set up in a **uniform**[50] way across the board to protect the royalty behind them. Most of the time, they only move one space forward at a time, unless there are **extenuating**[51] circumstances."

"So they're useless?" he said, throwing one off to the side.

"Hey! Don't you dare **presume**[52] anything and have some respect for these poor **ignoble**[53] pawns. They're the infantry and are very useful," Ashley said picking up the pawn and putting it on a spot.

"Sorry, I didn't mean to stoke your **ire**[54]," he said bowing to Ashley "or **imply**[55] that you had no purpose," he said with a bow to the pawn.

"He says you're forgiven. Now back to work, peasant!" Ashley said as she positioned the king.

---

[50] uniform (adj) always the same; (s) regular, consistent; (a) diverse

[51] extenuating (adj) partially excusing or justifying; (s) excusing, mitigating; (a) aggravating

[52] presume (v) take to be the case or to be true; (s) assume, suppose; (a) doubt

[53] ignoble (adj) not of the nobility; (s) lowly, inferior; (a) royal

[54] ire (n) belligerence aroused by a real or supposed wrong; (s) rage, fury; (a) cheer

[55] imply (v) express or state indirectly; (s) hint, suggest; (a) describe

"And this?" Josh picked up a bishop that was lying on its side. The shape of the bishop made it **cumbersome**[56] to carry and Josh seemed a bit **distressed**[57] with the awkwardness of it.

"That's a bishop. They go on the back row, third square from the end. They have to stay on their own color and are useful if you want to **facilitate**[58] a sneak attack because sometimes they're overlooked. I think it's because they blend in with the pawns."

"Then how do they catch pieces on the other color?" he asked.

"They don't. That's why you have to use all the different pieces on the board. Each one does something special. Like this one..." Ashley picked up a knight.

"It's a horse," Josh said.

"No, it's a knight. Oh my gosh, I get it! All it takes is a little **ingenuity**[59] and...the cross - that would be the king. He has a cross on his head. He stands next to the queen who always goes on her color. The horse - he's called a knight and he goes second from the end. He can move two up and one over. If you move the knight and bishop, and have the king on this side and the rook on the other

---

[56] cumbersome (adj) difficult to handle or use especially because of size or weight; (s) awkward, bulky; (a) handy

[57] distressed (adj) afflicted with or marked by anxious uneasiness or trouble or grief; (s) disturbed, unhappy; (a) carefree

[58] facilitate (v) make easier; (s) assist, help; (a) hinder

[59] ingenuity (n) the power of creative imagination; (s) skill, ability; (a) clumsiness

with nothing in between them, you do what's called a castle and swap them."

Ashley moved the pieces on the board as she explained what she was doing. Soon the rook and the king were next to each other.

"Now what?" Josh asked.

They scrambled to arrange the two pieces and them stood back to look at them. That's when Ashley saw it. A small glistening on the crown of the king. She moved in to take a closer look. It was a tiny plaque with an indentation of letters. It read, "God Morgon." Josh stood next to Ashley and got close to see what she was looking at. That's when a shine from the neck of the horse caught his eye. It was a small plaque that someone had used to **adorn**[60] the side of the horse near the harness. On the plaque was a **lily**[61] and in the center of it was the letter 'B'.

"Everywhere we go there's another 'B'. Boy, you Bonnys are everywhere, aren't you? Hey, what's that on the king's cross?" He read it. "God Morgon. He must not be that popular. He has to wear a name tag so everyone knows who he is." Josh laughed.

---

[60] adorn (v) make more attractive, as by adding ornament or color; (s) trim, grace; (a) blemish

[61] lily (n) any liliaceous plant of the genus Lilium having showy pendulous flowers; (s) layla, lila; (a) gladiator

"I don't think the 'B' stands for Bonny. Maybe it's a **metaphor**[62] for something else. They likely would **emboss**[63] it on his crown to **gratify**[64] his ego. And that's not his name. God Morgon is how you say good morning in Swedish. I learned that this morning in class. But what does it mean?"

Ashley was stumped. Something wasn't right and she knew it. She wondered if maybe the **collocation**[65] was wrong. She ran over to Josh's side and pushed the pieces he had set up out of the way.

"Hey!" he yelled. "I won't **concede**[66] the game before we even start."

"Think of finding the treasure as a **consolation**[67] prize. Come on. Help me castle the pieces on this side." Ashley moved the knight to a light square and castled the king and rook. "It's made another arrow. It's pointing at something."

"Wait, I recognize this." Josh was pointing at the **pinion**[68] with the 'B' on the breast of the horse. "It's a Linnea Borealis."

---

[62] metaphor (n) a figure of speech in which an expression is used to refer to something that it does not literally denote in order to suggest a similarity; (s) analogy, simile; (a) original

[63] emboss (v) raise in a relief; (s) impress, imprint; (a) disfigure

[64] gratify (v) make happy or satisfied; (s) please, indulge; (a) bully

[65] collocation (n) the act of positioning close together; (s) allocation, arrangement; (a) row

[66] concede (v) give over; (s) admit, allow; (a) deny

[67] consolation (n) the act of consoling; (s) cheer, satisfaction; (a) torment

[68] pinion (n) wing of a bird; (s) gable, quill; (a) separate

"A what?"

"A Linnea Borealis. It's an **agricultural**[69] term for a certain type of flower. My mom's a horticulturist and I've kind of been forced into learning lots of plants."

Ashley's face lit up. "This is a **tangible**[70] clue. I recognize that name from class this morning. If I remember right, it's the unofficial national flower of Sweden."

"It has to be a clue." Josh said. Josh knew it was another **milestone**[71] in their treasure hunt. He followed the line of the arrow made by the chess pieces with his eyes and they were pointing at the two elderly men playing chess at the small pop-up table and chairs. One of the men expressed great **consternation**[72] about his **dissent**[73] in the game while the other was very **convivial**[74]. Under their table was a patch of beautiful flowers. Josh recognized them instantly, ran past the chess pieces and over to the men.

---

[69] agricultural (adj) relating to rural matters; (s) rural, rustic; (a) urban

[70] tangible (adj) capable of being treated as fact; (s) material, real; (a) abstract

[71] milestone (n) a significant event in your life; (s) event, turning point; (a) failure

[72] consternation (n) fear resulting from the awareness of danger; (s) alarm, dismay; (a) calm

[73] dissent (n) a difference of opinion; (s) conflict, disagree; (a) assent

[74] convivial (adj) occupied with or fond of the pleasures of good company; (s) jolly, merry; (a) shy

"Maybe it's telling us to go to IKEA for meatballs? I love the way they **saturate**[75] them in the **savory**[76] sauce." Ashley being a little **sarcastic**[77] because the cookie and pastry was good, but her stomach had begun to grumble for some real food. She was determined not to let anything **hamper**[78] her search for the treasure, but as hard as she tried to ignore her growling stomach, it was to no **avail**[79]. She had always been a hearty eater and the donut and cookie were simply not enough to **satiate**[80] her appetite. She needed real food. She reached into her bag for a snack and found another letter sitting directly next to the carrots and **humus**[81]. On the outside was written:

READ ME WHEN YOU FIND THE TREASURE

Josh was watching the two men play chess, and Ashley was so hungry and **weary**[82] that she had become a bit **languid**[83] and a

---

[75] saturate (v) infuse or fill completely; (s) soak, drench; (a) dry

[76] savory (adj) having an agreeably pungent taste; (s) piquant, zesty; (a) insipid

[77] sarcastic (adj) expressing or expressive of ridicule that wounds; (s) ironic, satirical; (a) mild

[78] hamper (v) put at a disadvantage; (s) handicap, hinder; (a) assist

[79] avail (n) a means of serving; (s) help, service; (a) harm

[80] satiate (v) fill to satisfaction; (s) satisfy, gorge; (a) deprive

[81] humus (n) a thick spread made from mashed chickpeas, tahini, lemon juice and garlic; (s) humous; hummous; no antonym

[82] weary (adj) physically and mentally fatigued; (s) tired, exhausted; (a) energetic

[83] languid (adj) lacking spirit or liveliness; (s) sluggish, lethargic; (a) active

touch **pessimistic**[84]. It was not like Ashley to be a **pessimist**[85], but all she could think of was finding the treasure and getting some food. She wondered if the unopened letter would **disclose**[86] any information about where the treasure was and had to **deliberate**[87] carefully whether or not to open it. She stared at the envelope long and hard, testing herself and her integrity. Finally, she had to **resign**[88] herself to **adhere**[89] to the rules of the quest and put the letter back into her bag. She knew that finding the treasure was **doable**[90] without cheating.

Suddenly, Josh had an **epiphany**[91].

"The Fairy Gardens!"

---

[84] pessimistic (adj) expecting the worst possible outcome; (s) sad, glum; (a) rosy

[85] pessimist (n) a person who expects the worst; (s) gloomy, cynic; (a) dreamer

[86] disclose (v) expose to view as by removing a cover; (s) reveal, divulge; (a) hide

[87] deliberate (v) think about carefully; weigh; (s) ponder, consider; (a) hurried

[88] resign (v) accept as inevitable; (s) reconcile, submit; (a) agree

[89] adhere (v) follow through or carry out a plan without deviation; (s) observe, accede; (a) vacillate

[90] doable (adj) capable of being done; (s) viable, possible; (a) absurd

[91] epiphany (n) a divine manifestation; (s) discovery, revelation; (a) secret

Chapter 13

Ashley snapped out of her hunger.

"The Fairy Gardens?" she questioned as she ran to him. The two men playing chess glanced up at them and smiled. Ashley looked at the chess board on which contained the most magical and delightful chess pieces Ashley had ever seen. It was a fairy chess set. The top of the set was glass and it sat on four corner posts that looked like tree stumps. Below was an **idyllic**[1] fairyland with rocks and streams and magical hiding places where imaginary creatures lived lives filled with play and **folly**[2]. The chess figures were unicorns and fairies, dancing on the board in competitive laughter. It was as if the board could **foretell**[3] the future by showing them the way.

"There's an **outcropping**[4] of Linnea Borealis flowers blooming in the Fairy Gardens. They **flourish**[5] anywhere there's sun, but the **scarcity**[6] of where they grow in the garden should make them easy to find. Come on!" Josh said.

---

[1] idyllic (adj) excellent and delightful in all respects; (s) peaceful, ideal; (a) imperfect

[2] folly (n) a stupid mistake; (s) stupidity, foolishness; (a) wisdom

[3] foretell (v) foreshadow or presage; (s) announce, herald; (a) whisper

[4] outcropping (n) head or top of a plant; (s) crop, plant;

[5] flourish (v) grow vigorously; (s) boom, thrive; (a) fail

[6] scarcity (n) a small and inadequate amount; (s) lack, small; (a) plethora

The two men smiled and wished them good luck, they themselves being pirates and part of the treasure hunt.

Josh and Ashley ran out of the park and back into town. It was **fortuitous**[7] that Josh could figure out the next clue before Ashley let her hunger take over and she made the mistake of opening the letter. She would have felt awful cheating and she would have never forgiven herself for doing it. She was also happy that the next clue took them to the Fairy Gardens. It was one of her favorite places in the world.

The Fairy Gardens were a **whimsical**[8] place off the **cobble**[9] streets in the center of town. It was **composed**[10] of a large swath of grass mixed in with a **diversity**[11] of trees, flowers, butterflies, and tiny houses - all in miniature size. Long ago, it was a **arid**[12] dirt park with a wall around it that young people would **deface**[13] with

---

[7] fortuitous (adj) occurring by happy chance; (s) lucky, fluky; (a) unlucky

[8] whimsical (adj) odd or fantastic in appearance; quaintly devised; fantastic; (s) fantastic, fanciful; (a) normal

[9] cobble (n) rectangular paving stone with curved top; once used to make roads; (s) stones, sett; no antonym

[10] composed (v) to arrange in proper or orderly form; (s) collected, composes; (a) discomposed

[11] diversity (n) multiplicity of difference; (s) contrast, variety; (a) sameness

[12] arid (adj) lacking sufficient water or rainfall; (s) dry, barren; (a) humid

[13] deface (v) mar or spoil the appearance of; (s) vandalize, disfigure; (a) repair

spray paint and **desecrate**[14] with chalk, scrawling **detestable**[15] **profanity**[16] everywhere much to the **abject**[17] horror of the townspeople. The Mayor would publicly **condemn**[18] these actions, but no matter what the Mayor tried to do, no **deterrent**[19] would keep the hoodlums **compliant**[20] with the law. The Mayor saw how **detrimental**[21] it was to the beauty of the city, how it started to **devalue**[22] the neighborhood, and simply took out the wall to **abolish**[23] the graffiti, leaving the space **destitute**[24]. Weeds grew and the little plot of land began to **deteriorate**[25].

---

[14] desecrate (v) violate the sacred character of a place or language; (s) profane, defile; (a) bless

[15] detestable (adj) offensive to the mind; (s) odious, hateful: (a) good

[16] profanity (n) vulgar or irreverent speech or action; (s) impiety, swearing; (a) prudery

[17] abject (adj) most unfortunate or miserable; (s) low, wretched; (a) happy

[18] condemn (v) express strong disapproval of; (s) decry, excoriate; (a) approve

[19] deterrent (n) something immaterial that interferes with or delays action or progress; (s) hindrance, baulk; (a) help

[20] compliant (adj) yielding; (s) amenable, obedient; (a) stubborn

[21] detrimental (adj) causing harm or injury; (s) damaging, adverse; (a) beneficial

[22] devalue (v) lower the value or quality of; (s) depreciate, debase; (a) raise

[23] abolish (v) do away with; (s) eliminate, destroy; (a) support

[24] destitute (adj) completely wanting or lacking; (s) poor, penniless: (a) rich

[25] deteriorate (v) become worse or disintegrate; (s) decline, decay; (a) improve

But that didn't **stymie**[26] the creativity of those who wanted something better for this unused area in the center of town. Mr. Primpton, who was a very **proficient**[27] gardener, planted one small square garden with tiny figurines in the barren space. The people of the town loved his garden so much, each person added a little something to it until it grew and grew into kind of a central park. It was beyond beautiful, especially at this **autumnal**[28] time of year when everything was in bloom.

They ran past the ice cream shop owned by Mr. Downy, who was a bit of a **curmudgeon**[29], but his vanilla ice cream **bespoke**[30] genius. It was fresh and glorious because Mr. Downy would **grind**[31] his own vanilla beans! The ice cream shop was a **hub**[32] of action where girls and boys from all over town would **convene**[33]

---

[26] stymie (v) hinder or prevent the progress or accomplishment of; (s) block, obstruct; (a) help

[27] proficient (adj) having or showing knowledge and skill and aptitude; (s) adept, expert; (a) clumsy

[28] autumnal (adj) of or characteristic of or occurring in autumn; (s) fall, autumn; (a) wintry

[29] curmudgeon (n) a crusty irascible cantankerous old person full of stubborn ideas; (s) grouch, crank

[30] bespoke (adj) custom-made; (s) tailored, made-to-order; (a) standard

[31] grind (v) press or grind with a crushing noise; (s) crunch, crush; (a) free

[32] hub (n) a focal point around which events revolve; (s) focus, heart; (a) outside

[33] convene (v) meet formally; (s) assemble, gather; (a) adjourn

for socializing. The would stand **harmoniously**[34] outside and **vie**[35] for each other's attention, while the younger school kids were inside happily eating their hot fudge sundaes, banana splits, and whatever the new **craze**[36] there was for milk shakes. Anyone who looked inside could only **construe**[37] that this was a place of happiness.

Kenny Baker was standing out in front of the shop, performing his **habitual**[38] juggling of oranges to impress the girls. He was a **budding**[39] circus star, **ambidextrous**[40] which made him especially good at juggling, and he would juggle anything. He had extraordinary **dexterity**[41] and a smile that could **endear**[42] anyone. One time he tried to juggle three flaming sticks, but they had to **douse**[43] them out when they caught fire to his hair. He didn't need

[34] harmoniously (adv) in a harmonious manner; (s) agreeably, kindly; (a) grimly

[35] vie (v) compete for something; (s) contend, compete; (a) collaborate

[36] craze (n) a temporary passion or infatuation; (s) rage, fad; (a) balance

[37] construe (v) make sense of; (s) interpret, explain; (a) confuse

[38] habitual (n) according to habit; (s) regular, usual; (a) unusual

[39] budding (adj) beginning to develop; (s) beginning, burgeoning; (a) dying

[40] ambidextrous (adj) equally skillful with each hand; (s) skillful, able; (a) dextral

[41] dexterity (n) skill and ease in using the hands; (s) skill, ability; (a) clumsiness

[42] endear (v) make attractive or lovable; (s) charm, captivate; (a) alienate

[43] douse (v) wet thoroughly; (s) drench, soak; (a) dry

any special **apparatus**[44], he only needed various objects that would be easy enough to grasp.

The **enigmatic**[45] Pete Moran was leaning against the wall in his stately **chapeaux**[46] (as he called it). He was in the Drama Club and wore a top hat everywhere. Some of the kids thought he was bald underneath because no one had ever seen him without his hat.

They hurried in front of the bus drivers who were sitting in their running buses under the trees to shade them from the **harshness**[47] of the afternoon sun, the **acrid**[48] smell of the **corrosive**[49] exhaust billowing into the street, while the driver's sat comfortably in the driver's seats watching sports videos on their cell phones. Their bosses would soon call and to **rouse**[50] them from the comfort of their break time to return to their jobs.

They ran past the dry cleaners, owned by an **entrepreneur**[51] who also owned the convenience store, until they finally reached

---

[44] apparatus (n) equipment designed to serve a specific function; (s) device, gear; (a) balk

[45] enigmatic (adj) not clear to the understanding; (s) puzzling, mysterious; (a) clear

[46] chapeaux (n) hat or cap; (s) fedoras, caps; no antonyms

[47] harshness (n) the quality of being unpleasant; (s) severity, cruelty; (a) softness

[48] acrid (adj) causing heat and irritation; (s) nasty, hot; (a) sweet

[49] corrosive (adj) eating away; (s) corroding, erosive; (a) fortifying

[50] rouse (v) cause to become awake or conscious; (s) move, inspire; (a) lull

[51] entrepreneur (n) someone who organizes a business venture and assumes the risk for it; (s) manager, contractor; (a) employee

City Hall where they turned left and saw the Fairy Gardens in the town square. The gardens were lit up with **adequate**[52] sunlight and they were hoping that finding where they needed to go wasn't too difficult. They ran past the butterfly **sanctuary**[53], then the **aviary**[54] and into the garden, which was in full bloom. It was a glorious, **homogeneous**[55] mix of plants, trees, and flowers.

"This is the spot I was thinking of, but everything's covered in twinflowers. The caretaker must have planted more this year. Now I don't know where to look," said Josh.

They were facing a **conundrum**[56]. Normally, Ashley wouldn't hesitate to ask the **benevolent**[57] caretaker to **enlighten**[58] her about certain plants and where to find them, but he was on an **ephemeral**[59] **hiatus**[60] in Bermuda. He was a **prolific**[61] gardener

---

[52] adequate (adj) sufficient for the purpose; (s) sufficient, enough; (a) shy

[53] sanctuary (n) a shelter from danger or hardship; (s) refuge, haven; (a) trap

[54] aviary (n) a building where birds are kept; (s) volary, birdhouse; no antonyms

[55] homogeneous (adj) all of the same or similar kind or nature; (s) same; uniform; (a) diverse

[56] conundrum (n) a difficult problem; (s) riddle, enigma; (a) answer

[57] benevolent (adj) generous in providing aid to others; (s) kind charitable; (a) selfish

[58] enlighten (v) make free from confusion or ambiguity; (s) inform, illuminate; (a) confuse

[59] ephemeral (adj) lasting a very short time; (s) brief, fleeting; (a) permanent

[60] hiatus (n) an interruption in the intensity or amount of something; (s) break, respite; (a) continuation

[61] prolific (adj) Intellectually productive; (s) abundant, fruitful; (a) jejune

who had two green thumbs. His prowess with greenery was **enviable**[62] and there were few other people in town they would **entrust**[63] to care for the Fairy Gardens. She leaned on his empty cart as kind of an **homage**[64] to him, secretly hoping he was enjoying his beach time. Looking around, she struggled to find the next clue and then remembered the map given to her by Aunt Tessie. She took it out of her bag.

"I have a treasure map," she said.

"And why didn't you pull this out earlier?" Josh said.

"Because we didn't need it earlier. Come on, admit it. This was fun and looking at this map earlier would have **dissipated**[65] some of that fun."

"You're right. So where we do we go, captain?" Josh said with a **salute**[66].

---

[62] enviable (adj) causing envy; (s) desired,lucky; (a) unlucky
[63] entrust (v) confer a trust upon; (s) assign, charge; (a) keep
[64] homage (n) respectful deference; (s) worship, praise; (a) scorn
[65] dissipate (v) to cause to separate and go in different directions; (s) waste, squander; (a) hoard
[66] salute (v) express commendation of; (s) honor, saluting: (a) ignore

Since Ashley had a treasure map, Josh was now her **subordinate**[67] and **submissive**[68] to her commands. Ashley looked at the map and tried to get her bearings.

"Even if we had taken this out earlier, I doubt it would have done us any good. It's pretty **cryptic**[69]. Why couldn't they make it easy and **coherent**[70]?"

Josh looked over her shoulder and with all the **diplomacy**[71] he could muster he said, "That's how pirate maps are supposed to be; otherwise, anyone can find the treasure."

"This is definitely the Fairy Gardens. Look, this is Mrs. Anderson's section with the green gnomes and trolls with the **tawny**[72] hair."

Josh pointed to another place on the map. "I recognize this spot. It's where Mrs. Smythe put that **hideous**[73] looking tree with

---

[67] subordinate (n) an assistant subject to the authority or control of another; (s) junior, lower; (a) boss

[68] submissive (adj) showing a readiness to submit; (s) yielding, compliant; (a) royal

[69] cryptic (adj) of an obscure nature; (s) obscure, mysterious; (a) obvious

[70] coherent (adj) marked by an orderly, logical, and aesthetically consistent relation of parts; (s) lucid, orderly; (a) irrational

[71] diplomacy (n) subtly skillful handling of a situation; (s) discretion, tact; (a) rudeness

[72] tawny (adj) of a light brown to brownish orange color; (s) brown, tan; (a) black

[73] hideous (adj) grossly offensive to decency or morality; (s)

all the **sap**[74]. You know, the one that looks like a cross between something out of Alien and Whoville."

Mrs Smythe was a **homely**[75] woman who used any means she could to dress up the world around her.

"Look at this," Ashley said as she pointed to a tiny 'x'. Ashley smiled. "I know where the treasure is. Why didn't I think of it before? Let's go to the top of the hill where we can get an **aerial**[76] view of the gardens."

They ran to the top of the hill and looked out over the gardens. It only took Ashley a moment to **acclimate**[77] herself to where she was and where they had to go. She had been here many times with Aunt Tessie who had a particular **affinity**[78] for this very special place in the gardens. She should have known where the treasure would have been hidden.

---

[74] sap (n) a watery solution of sugars, salts, and minerals that circulates through the vascular system of a plant; (s) milk, juice; (a) water
[75] homely (adj) lacking in physical beauty or proportion; (s) plain, ugly; (a) beautiful
[76] aerial (adj) of or pertaining to the air or atmosphere; (s) elevated, overhead; (a) ground
[77] acclimate (v) get used to a certain environment; (s) adapt, adjust; (a) muddle
[78] affinity (n) a natural attraction or feeling of kinship; (s) attraction, rapport; (a) dislike

They walked down an **esoteric**[79] stone path, through the tiny vines and **willowy**[80] trees that amazed them with their **ethereal**[81] beauty. They crossed over the wooden bridge that led into a miniature village filled with huts and little stone walls. They passed the tree where the Mayor of the Fairy Gardens kept watch from his perch high (well, high for tiny fairies) above the land. They even passed the hippie fairies with an old, **dilapidated**[82] miniature VW Bus that had been put there by Grace Rosebud, the town hippie.

Ashley stopped at the far side of the garden on the edge of a **quagmire**[83] where there was a tiny willow tree identical to the one where she met Josh. Next to the tree was a winding **ceramic**[84] stream, just like the stream next to the tree where Josh had been sitting. And in the stream was a **vessel**[85], brilliant and **buoyant**[86] in the water. It was a small but stately pirate ship, proudly waving the pirate flag, and captained by a small pirate fairy at the helm.

---

[79] esoteric (adj) marked by secrecy or privacy; (s) secret, occult; (a) known

[80] willowy (adj) slender and graceful; (s) slim, svelte; (a) fat

[81] ethereal (adj) of heaven or the spirit; (s) celestial, airy; (a) earthy

[82] dilapidated (adj) in deplorable condition; (s) shabby, decayed; (a) new

[83] quagmire (n) a soft wet area of low-lying land that sinks underfoot; (s) marsh, bog; (a) desert

[84] ceramic (n) an artifact made of clay baked at a high temperature; (s) pottery, china; no antonym

[85] vessel (n) a craft designed for water transportation; (s) boat, ship; (a) eject

[86] buoyant (adj) tending to float on a liquid or rise in air or gas; (s) floaty; (a) sink

"**Cease-fire**[87]! They be friendly pirates!" yelled Josh behind Ashley. Ashley smiled and laughed.

"It's got to be here," Ashley said as she looked at the map. Josh reached down and lifted up the pirate ship.

"Pirate Roberts reporting for duty," he joked.

The ship was wooden and had three masts with sails fully unfurled to make it look as if it was sailing the high seas. A tiny black pirate flag with skull, crossbones and a small 'B' proudly flew atop of the mast. Josh set the ship back down and looked at Ashley with a sense of pride.

"According to the map, we dig here," Ashley said, pointing to the tiny 'x' on the map. "There, just below the willow tree."

"That tiny little spot has our gold?" Josh asked with a bit of disappointment. "Oh well."

He pulled a hand shovel out of his backpack and began to **excavate**[88] next to the little tree. He dug and dug and dug, until a small treasure chest appeared. It was not a **mirage**[89], but a true

---

[87] Cease-fire (n) a state of peace agreed to between opponents so they can discuss peace terms; (s) truce; peace; (a) war

[88] excavate (v) recover through digging; (s) unearth, mine; (a) bury

[89] mirage (n) optical illusion in which hot air distorts distant objects; (s) illusion, vision; (a) reality

miniature pirate's treasure chest. It was the **pinnacle**[90] of their quest.

"Well, what do you know?" said Josh. He picked up the miniature chest and held it out to Ashley. "You're the lead pirate. Open it."

Ashley took the tiny chest into her hands and lifted the top. Inside were two tiny gold coins. She turned over the chest and dumped the coins into her hand. One coin had the symbol for the pirate Bartholomew Roberts and the other had a symbol for Anne Bonny. She handed the Roberts coin to Josh.

"I shall **administer**[91] the officiation." Ashley cleared her throat and formally held out the coin. "It's official. You, Josh Roberts, have now earned the **moniker**[92] of a Roberts pirate," she said proudly.

Josh took the other coin and held it out for Ashley.

"It's official. You, Ash Bonny, have now earned the moniker of a Bonny pirate," he said proudly.

---

[90] pinnacle (n) the highest level or degree attainable; (s) peak, apex; (a) nadir

[91] administer (v) administer or bestow, as in small portions; (s) manage, control; (a) neglect

[92] moniker (n) a familiar name for a person; (s) title, nickname; (a) superscript

Ashley looked back at the **progress**[93] of the day. She never thought she would arrive at this moment here after her initial **blunder**[94] of not reading the letter, but here she was - a pirate. It was a **pivotal**[95] moment in Ashley's life and one that she would never forget.

They looked at each other for a moment, not knowing what to do next. They burst into laughter and began to dance around, almost giddy with delight. They danced with **lunacy**[96] and exuberance, joyful in succeeding in their adventure. Then Ashley remembered the envelope. She reached into her bag and took out the envelope, hoping it would not be another riddle to **bewilder**[97] them. She opened the envelope, and inside was a letter and another envelope. She unfolded the letter and read it out loud:

> IF YOU ARE READING THIS LETTER, IT MEANS THAT YOU HAVE FOUND THE TREASURE AND COMPLETED YOUR TASK OF BECOMING AN OFFICIAL PIRATE. CONGRATULATIONS! TODAY YOU START A

---

[93] progress (n) gradual improvement or growth or development; (s) advance, develop; (a) decline

[94] blunder (n) an embarrassing mistake; (s) mistake, error; (a) accuracy

[95] pivotal (adj) being of crucial importance; (s) crucial, central; (a) minor

[96] lunacy (n) foolish or senseless behavior; (s) insanity, madness; (a) saneness

[97] bewilder (v) be a mystery or bewildering to; (s) confuse, perplex; (a) clarify

LEGACY FOR THE NEXT GENERATION OF PIRATES. OPEN THE LAST ENVELOPE AND CELEBRATE WITH ICE CREAM.

Josh pulled an envelope out of his backpack and opened it. He was going to read an **excerpt**[98] from it, but realized the two letters were identical.

"It's the same," he said.

They both opened the other envelopes and, in a **bizarre**[99] twist, inside were two one hundred dollar bills. Josh's were stamped with an 'R' and Ashley's were stamped with a 'B'. It was a **culmination**[100] of their efforts of the day. The **brevity**[101] of the day left them longing for more adventures, but they were both immensely proud of their **triumph**[102] in following the clues and becoming pirates. This was not a **trivial**[103] moment and they knew it. It was special.

"Well, it really does pay to be a pirate," said Ashley.

---

[98] excerpt (n) a passage selected from a larger work; (s) quote, passage; (a) whole

[99] bizarre (adj) conspicuously or grossly unconventional or unusual; (s) strange, weird; (a) normal

[100] culmination (n) a concluding action; (s) peak, climax; (a) beginning

[101] brevity (n) the attribute of being short or fleeting; (s) briefness, shortness; (a) longevity

[102] triumph (n) a successful ending of a struggle or contest; (s) win, victory; (a) victory

[103] trivial (adj) (informal) small and of little importance; (s) minor, unimportant; (a) significant

"What's you favorite, vanilla or chocolate?" asked Josh.

"Pirate's **Bounty**[104]," she said with a smile.

---

[104] bounty (n) the property of copious abundance; (s) reward, premium;
(a) avarice, absence

Chapter 14

Through their **cumulative**[1] efforts, as well as being **observant**[2] and cunning, Josh and Ashley had competed their mission. They swore to remain the best of friends in **perpetuity**[3] and always have each other's back. They also agreed to be **steadfast**[4] in their pursuit of changing the **stereotype**[5] of pirates and showing the world their value.

Josh went home to celebrate with his family. Ashley headed back to the school, picked up her bike and rode to Aunt Tessie's house. Aunt Tessie was waiting in the doorway to greet her with a look of pure **reverence**[6] on her face. Ashley dropped her bike in the grass and ran to give her Aunt Tessie a huge hug.

"I'm proud of you, child. You have gone through a wondrous **metamorphosis**[7] today to **ameliorate**[8] yourself. You worked well

---

[1] cumulative (adj) Increasing by successive addition; (s) additive, increasing; (a) declining

[2] observant (adj) quick to notice; (s) alert, watchful; (a) careless

[3] perpetuity (n) the property of being perpetual (seemingly ceaseless); (s) eternity, infinity; (a) end

[4] steadfast (adj) firm and dependable especially in loyalty; (s) staunch, unswerving; (a)

[5] stereotype (n) a conventional or formulaic conception or image; (s) stamp, cliche; (s) new

[6] reverence (n) a feeling of profound respect for someone or something; (s) respect,worship; (a) scorn

[7] metamorphosis (n) a striking change in appearance or character or circumstances; (s) change, shift; (a) regular

[8] ameliorate (v) to make better; (s) improve, upgrade; (a) worsen

with Josh to **decode**[9] the clues and didn't cheat. Being a true **intellectual**[10], you used your power of **deduction**[11] to complete your quest. You've earned the title of Ash Bonny and I would **deem**[12] you to be a true pirate. I cannot **ingrain**[13] into you enough how important this is."

Aunt Tessie reached into her pocket, pulled out a small pin and pinned it to Ashley's shirt. It was the symbol for the Bonny Pirates and had the letters 'AB' on it.

"I knew you could do it," Aunt Tessie said as she kissed Ashley's forehead.

"There was no **parallel**[14] to anything like this I've ever done in my entire life. It was super fun - with a big **emphasis**[15] on the word fun - and I can't wait to learn everything there is to know about our family."

---

[9] decode (v) convert code into ordinary language; (s) decrypt, decipher; (a) encode

[10] intellectual (n) a person who uses the mind creatively; (s) genius, mental; (a) ignorant

[11] deduction (n) reasoning from the general to the particular; (s) reasoning, synthesis; (a) addition

[12] deem (v) to account; (s) think, judge; (a) ignore

[13] ingrain (v) thoroughly work in; (s) fix, root; (a) off

[14] parallel (adj) being everywhere equidistant and not intersecting; (s) compare, equal; (a) crooked

[15] emphasis (n) Intensity or forcefulness of expression; (s) stress, priority; (a) weakness

"Being a pirate can mean leading a **desolate**[16] life, but don't let that **deter**[17] you. It has its rewards too. I'm glad you thought it was fun because I have another task for you. One of the other pirates is in **peril**[18] and needs a hand. I've volunteered you to help. Are you up for the task?"

Ashley was so excited she almost burst.

"Of course. I'm a Bonny Pirate, never to **cower**[19] from a challenge and always ready to take on any **perilous**[20] task. It's the pirate's **creed**[21]. What do I have to do?"

"Come inside and you can start in the morning."

Aunt Tessie didn't have to be **emphatic**[22] this time about starting tomorrow. This time Ashley was able to be patient and **discerning**[23] because she knew that she would **endure**[24] the night and tomorrow's adventure would be well worth the wait. All fear

---

[16] desolate (adj) providing no shelter or sustenance; (s) lonely, dismal; (a) cheerful

[17] deter (v) try to prevent; (s) dissuade, prevent; (a) encourage

[18] peril (n) a state of danger involving risk; (s) hazard, risk; (a) safety

[19] cower (v) show submission or fear; (s) cringe, shrink; (a) face

[20] perilous (adj) fraught with danger; (s) risky, dangerous; (a) safe

[21] creed (n) a set of beliefs or aims that guide someone's actions; (s) belief, credo; (a) betrayal

[22] emphatic (adj) forceful and definite in expression or action; (s) firm, assertive; (a) faint

[23] discerning (adj) unobtrusively perceptive and sympathetic; (s) shrewd, clever; (a) crazy

[24] endure (v) put up with something or somebody unpleasant; (s) last, bear; (a) enjoy

of herself as a pirate had **dissolved**[25] and it was difficult not to be **effusive**[26] about the next quest. She nodded in agreement to her Aunt and started to walk into the house, but stopped in the doorway. She turned to her Aunt Tessie.

"Can Josh help?" she said hopefully. She knew that his **insightful**[27] **erudition**[28] would be invaluable.

Aunt Tessie smiled. "He'll be here first thing in the morning. Now, come on. I've made your favorite, pot roast. You must be famished."

Ashley was hungry. Very hungry. The **meager**[29] amount of food she had consumed throughout the day was not enough on which to **thrive**[30]. It had been a long and exciting day, one which caused a **subtle**[31] change in Ashley. Where once was a girl who was **apprehensive**[32] about taking risks, there was now an

---

[25] dissolved (v) close down or dismiss; (s) disband, dismiss; (a) bind

[26] effusive (adj) uttered with unrestrained enthusiasm; (s) gushy, gushing; (a) detached

[27] insightful (adj) exhibiting insight or clear and deep perception; (s) perceptive, astute; (a) dumb

[28] erudition (n) profound scholarly knowledge; (s) learning, teaching; (a) insanity

[29] meager (adj) deficient in amount or quality or extent; (s) slight, scanty; (a) plentiful

[30] thrive (v) grow vigorously; (s) flourish, succeed; (a) fail

[31] subtle (adj) difficult to detect or grasp by the mind or analyze; (s) astute, sly; (a) obvious

[32] apprehensive (adj) in fear or dread of possible evil or harm; (s) nervous, anxious; (a) calm

adventurer who could **assert**[33] herself in any situation. She was no longer a **charlatan**[34], but a real Bonny Pirate. And she earned it. It wasn't garnered through **chicanery**[35] or cheating. It was earned and there was no anxiety left - only the **clarity**[36] of how special this honor was.

After giving Aunt Tessie a brief **synopsis**[37] of the day's events, Ashley went into the room and began to write her own pirate **memoir**[38]. She would go to bed to have **lavish**[39] adventuresome dreams that would **liberate**[40] her spirit, only to wake tomorrow heading into a **subsequent**[41] adventure. Ash Bonny didn't know how **prominent**[42] she would become in the pirate world, but she would soon find out that she was going to have a **profuse**[43] amount of adventures in an entirely new realm. No longer would she lead a

---

[33] assert (v) in fear or dread of possible evil or harm; (s) affirm, declare; (a) deny

[34] charlatan (n) a flamboyant deceiver; (s) fraud, cheat; (a) honesty

[35] chicanery (n) the use of tricks to deceive someone; (s) trickery, deception; (a) good

[36] clarity (n) free from obscurity and easy to understand; (s) clearness, distinctness; (a) confusion

[37] synopsis (n) a sketchy summary of the main points of an argument or theory; (s) outline, digest; (a) explain

[38] memoir (n) an account of the author's personal experiences; (s) journal, account; (a) fantasy

[39] lavish (adj) very generous; (s) profuse, splendid; (a) poor

[40] liberate (v) grant freedom to; (s) release, free; (a) restrain

[41] subsequent (adj) following in time or order; (s) after, future; (a) previous

[42] prominent (adj) having a quality that thrusts itself into attention; (s) eminent, famous; (a) invisible

[43] profuse (adj) superabundant; (s) copious, lavish; (a) sparse

fallow[44] life, but one of great adventure[45]. She would become

hooked[46] on the pirate's life and was **destined**[47] for greatness

because the world had a need for the pirate, Ash Bonny.

---

[44] fallow (adj) undeveloped but potentially useful; (s) inactive, uncultivated; (a) developed

[45] infamy (n) evil fame or public reputation; (s) notoriety, stigma; (a) innocence

[46] hooked (adj) addicted to; (s) crooked, addicted; (a) calm

[47] destined (adj) headed or intending to head in a certain direction; (s) fated, predestined; (a) born

Made in the USA
Middletown, DE
10 May 2021